Honorée Corder
Author, *Vision to Reality*

Business Dating
Applying Relationship Rules in
Business for Ultimate Success

Published by Honorée Enterprises Publishing, LLC

ISBN: 978-0-9961861-0-0

Discover other titles by Honorée Corder at
http://www.HonoreeCorder.com.

Table of Contents

BUSINESS DATING

Dear Reader,

You wouldn't start a conversation with a new love interest like this: *"Hello. Nice to meet you. Please take off your pants."* In essence that's what a lot of people do in business, and yet, there's so much more to relationship development than that. Some individuals spend a short time with someone, over coffee or in their office, and then after a brief conversation, expect to be hired or referred, and introductions immediately made.

By all accounts, this is the expectation after most initial meetings. We meet someone new, explain what we do, and then expect them to send us an endless stream of business *without ever taking the time to develop a relationship.* Does this sound familiar? Oh, wait, of course *you'd* never do that, but I'm sure you're thinking of someone you have met who has done exactly that recently. I know I am.

Business Dating is much like personal relationship dating. You can only reap the true and best rewards of a deep relationship when enough time has passed to develop that type of relationship.

In *Business Dating,* I draw parallels between personal and professional dating, making the case for why and how you should invest your time—indeed your most precious resource. Developing deep, meaningful, and long-lasting relationships with a select group of other professionals that will yield for you everything you could possibly hope for, personally and professionally, and so much more.

Business Dating further clarifies what great networking can be like, and ultimately get you going in the right direction! Are you ready? Let's go! To your best success!

Honorée Corder
Visionary, Strategist, Writer, Coach, Wife, Mom

PROLOGUE

Who am I?

I'm an author, executive business coach, speaker and corporate trainer, friend, wife, mom, and above all, an optimist.

In my work as an executive and business coach, I work with senior level professionals, entrepreneurs, and business owners from all backgrounds and education levels.

Over the past seventeen years, my clients have all been very nice people who wanted *more*—more income, revenue, clients, customers and time. I address all but the last one in this book.

I barely graduated from high school and didn't attend college, so I didn't have access to sorority sisters, private, law, or business school buddies, or outstanding alumni hook-ups, nor did my parents run large corporations, have decades-long friendships, or golfing buddies that could help me.

Before you pull out the smallest violin and play *"My Heart Cries for You,"* no worries. My life, career and businesses have all turned out just fine because I studied, implemented, and cracked the code on creating a network *from scratch*. In fact, I've done so multiple times, in major cities and small communities, each time without an ace up my sleeve.

I studied, taught and refined relationship and business development over the past two decades. Given my self-taught expertise, I'm excited to share with you what I've learned so you, too, can build a network that serves you in every way, both personally and professionally.

Who are you?

You are a competent, friendly, professional who sometimes struggles with building your network. You would love to have a "referral-only" business, which means you'll sit in the enviable chair of having daily referrals come to you, while not having to go to networking event after networking event in the hopes of meeting the right people.

You might be new to the business world and have a fledgling network of fellow college, law or business school graduates {who aren't exactly networking geniuses}, but you don't know what to do with those connections. Or perhaps you may have twenty-five years of experience {as is the case of many of my clients}, yet still have to stress year after year about how to make your numbers and wonder where business is going to come from. I assume you certainly want to avoid interactions like the one I shared in the Introduction, right? I know, me too!

Sometimes bad business dates are unavoidable, but for the most part you can ensure frustrating and unsatisfying meetings are few and far between utilizing the simple and straightforward strategies and techniques in this book.

Regardless of where you are today, tomorrow holds great promise because you're holding a guide with the how-to, when-to, why-to, and with who spelled out. How would you feel if there were no more guessing or stressing about developing business relationships and/or wondering how to monetize them in the right way, at the right time, and with the right people?

You would feel great, and that's exactly how you're going to feel at the end of this book: great!

Shall we? Let's do this!

Chapter One:
What is Business Dating?

In personal dating, two people spend time together to determine what, if anything, they have in common. They break bread, attend events, and talk to each other as they individually determine if the person they are with is someone they want to get to know better (and perhaps potentially marry), get to know on a limited basis, or cross off the list altogether.

Business dating is much like personal dating. Every day in business, we meet people who potentially could be clients or customers, utilize as strategic partners, or determine they are someone we would neither hire, have as client, nor refer to our networks.

Like personal dating, the best business dating relationships are often long-term "romances."

A great relationship, professional or personal, also lives in a perpetual state of win-win. It is mutually beneficial, high-trust, and boasts a large amount of "I'm so lucky to know you, what can I do for you today?" contained within it.

The exact same elements that go into building a successful and fruitful *personal* relationship go into building a successful and fruitful *professional* relationship. There's a choice to be made by each relationship seeker. Perhaps they want a quick-and-dirty, very short term and limited association, a contact that is pleasant yet avoids engaging in a business relationship and is mostly transactional? In a traditional relationship, this is called a one-night stand.

Or maybe there is a desire for a mutually beneficial, meaningful connection, complete with a lifetime of happiness? We honor these as the couples who celebrate their 50th wedding anniversary, with children and grandchildren in tow.

I'll do my best to avoid being crass or gauche throughout this book, yet we all identify with personal dating and relationships, the aforementioned one-night stands, or relationships of convenience. Then there are also symbiotic relationships that equally meet the needs of both parties, last a long time, and are mutually beneficial.

This book is about creating a plethora of the latter.

In business, there are people who treat their relationships as though they are one-night stands: *I don't need to know your name; I just want your cash.*

There are connections people have with others that are strictly transactional in nature: *I provide you with a product or service, you provide me with payment.*

The best business relationships I've seen and experienced involve two people who genuinely care about each other, are built on a solid time-tested foundation, and have the added benefit of the sale of products and services.

BUSINESS DATING

I'll let you and your imagination run wild as I draw comparisons between the two, hopefully causing you to think while not offending you. I'll assume you've never had a one-night stand (personal or professional), while withholding judgment if you have.

If you're happily married, you most likely know what I mean when I talk about a cooperative and supportive relationship. Perhaps you can think back to a time when you experienced a one-night stand. If you've had one, that is. Imagine you *have* if you haven't. No need to raise your hand; our discussion about this scenario requires no disclosure and is not about whether you've actually had a one-night stand. Your job is to imagine {or remember} what you think it might feel like the next morning, to be the one who is used, never to be called again, and go on with your life.

In business, if you've built something for yourself, most likely you've done so surrounded by excellent people who use and love your products and services, and also share about them, and you, with the world. Even if you're a solo practitioner, all of your business didn't just roll in the door because you once hung out a shingle. In addition to being intentional and purposeful about building your network, it took cooperation, communication, and compromise. Building your career took determination, caring, and most likely a group of people who believed in you, hired you, and referred you to others because they knew you, liked you, and trusted you. Your business in all probability wasn't built on a string of one-off experiences, quick encounters, and single sales. I know this is true because those don't come close to building a strong business that is both profitable and sustaining.

*Networking is like dating. When it's done
right, it is amazing. When done wrong, it's
like literally living a bad movie.*

The Vision

The question of the day for you is: "What do you
really want from your business relationships?" If
you're the type of person that goes from person to
person, business-to-business, and transaction-to-
transaction without a care or concern for the people
you're doing business with, *stop reading and return
this book.* It simply isn't for you. Pass it on to your
caring but more socially challenged brothers and
sisters who want a chance at the sterling status of
success that can only be had by someone who actually
cares about the people they meet every day in
business.

If, on the other hand, you've often wondered how
to develop long-term, mutually-beneficial and
revenue-generating relationships that cause your
business to grow month-over-month, year-over-year,
decade-over-decade, and you genuinely care for the
other guy, this is the book for you.

Becoming a successful networker, no, indeed a
successful *rainmaker*, honestly requires a skill set you
most likely don't already have. Let's face it, you most
likely wouldn't be reading this book if you already
had a super-busy career with plenty of revenue and a
tight network that referred you business every single
day. (That is, of course, unless you're a .01%-er ...
someone who is always looking to be "that much
better." My hat is off to you, then, and thanks so much
for reading.)

Listen, in a great economy, your business is only
as strong as your strongest relationships. In a bad

economy, your business is only as strong as your strongest relationships. The difference is, in a good economy, you'll find it much easier to find customers and clients. Since we're waist-deep in a down economy with no end in sight, many people are slowly dying in the quick-sand pit called "Almost Out of Business" because they don't know what networking to do, with whom, when to do it, or even *why to do it.*

It's just like the daters out there who are dating for the sport of dating. They are the players, the "one-and-done-ers" who flit like butterflies leaving a wake of confusion and broken hearts. Perhaps they, too, want a mutually beneficial long-term relationship, however they don't know what networking to do, with whom, when to do it, or even *why to do it.* It doesn't matter about the players and the casual daters, but for the business folks who want to do better, there is certainly a better, and dare I say *easier,* way.

Just like the folks I will tell you about in an upcoming chapter, these same people smell of desperation, setting up meetings where they employ tactics from the Spanish Inquisition, and then almost demand introductions.

If you're like me, you see examples of successful "business dating," also known as networking, every day. When I talk to my clients, strategic partners and friends, they tell me about the new referral they got from a networking group, a call from a client with the name of a relative that needs their services, or an inquiry from someone they knew in school. They report new business coming in the door on a regular basis. When they need something, they put out the word, or simply pick up the phone and reach out to a few, close relationships. If you've watched this in action, it seems effortless and easy. Networking is only easy in the fact you can easily draw the conclusion that it's easy. But is it really? Yes, and not so much.

In my fifteen years as an executive coach, and over twenty years as a business dater, I've observed some pretty interesting behaviors, and heard some interesting dictums.

I've heard: "ABC – Always Be Closing."

Has someone tried to "close" you? Can you recall a time when ventured out in search of a possible purchase, only to be "closed," which you may or may not be entirely thrilled about, then have the sales person ask you for the names of five people you think would benefit from being contacted? That's the extreme. A tad more subtle is the dater/networker/salesy-slickster who sits with you, makes small talk, and then dives into what they do. Finally, they close the conversation with, "So, who manages your money?" and "If you know any millionaires who need to invest their money, I'd surely love to have an introduction." Umm, *no*.

Then there's: "Always ask for introductions."

Sales programs typically include some variation of "find out who they know and get an introduction right away."

I met a woman named Deb[*] some years ago who clearly abided by these two principles of *always be closing* and *get introductions*. She was, and is to this

---

[*] Names in this book have been changed to protect the innocent, socially inept, or guilty.

day, with a high-end investment firm. Some of her clients include the wealthiest individuals and families in town, and she's done very well for herself. I love to meet other successful professionals, and was thrilled to have the opportunity to schedule an appointment to meet with her.

We met over coffee, where she proceeded to spend the entire hour telling me about her business, who her clients were, what type of new clients she was looking for, and all about her daughter's upcoming wedding. She didn't ask me a single question about my business or inquire at all about my life, family, business, or interests. But she sure did ask me for introductions to a few close friends of mine she knew of by name but didn't know personally.

I left that meeting very clear about Deb: she was a *taker*. She wanted into my network and she knew she wanted into my network. I'm sure she did what she'd been taught to do: tell what you do and ask for introductions. But during our first meeting it was way too premature to make that ask, and all she did was send me running in the opposite direction with a bad taste in my mouth.

What could have been a fantastic mutually beneficial relationship and collaboration ended as quickly as it began. Full-access just doesn't happen on the first date, and if it does, it feels dirty and at least one person feels used and discarded.

Months later, a mutual acquaintance told me she felt like she'd wasted an hour of her life meeting with me because I hadn't made any introductions and she hadn't heard from me.

Duh.

I left feeling like I'd had a bad first date, and never called her again. She left feeling like she'd "put in her time" and wanted something back right away. Do you see the difference? Perhaps you're nodding your head and understanding now why some people have never called you back, or on the flip side, remembering times when you've been in my chair.

What most sales and networking training fails to do is truly educate people how to ask the questions necessary to get to know the person in front of them, during multiple meetings, over time. We aren't necessarily taught to find out if we actually like, or could like, our new contact. Yet, if you don't take the time to ask the right questions, how do you know if the person across the table is a potential prospect, strategic partner, friend or none of the above?

What I'm referencing is the difference between being effective and ineffective. Effective business dating yields more of what everyone wants, less of what they don't. Ineffective business dating is frustrating and leaves individuals wanting much, much more. Yet, the differences between effective and ineffective business dating aren't always huge, in fact, they are mere inches apart in some cases. In others, they are indeed miles apart.

Let's not belabor the point or point fingers, in fact, that's not what I'm trying to do at all. Everyone has countless stories of bad business dates, and although they can be most amusing, spending time on what's happened before today won't get you more of what you want now and in the future unless they are used as an opportunity to learn and improve. To that end, examples used will only be for the purposes of schooling you so you may grow as a networker.

As a coach I live in the world of "effective or ineffective" vs. "right or wrong." No judgment here, I'm just providing true and valuable information that can change your life for the better, and at the same time, fatten up that skinny wallet you're carrying around.

Let's Do This ... Right

What do the successful rainmakers have that unsuccessful bad business daters don't? It's not always what they *have*, it's what they've *had:* a model.

Let's use Melanie Birmingham as an example. Melanie grew up in a town in the Midwest with educators for parents, and was one of only two children, known for their shy tendencies. As luck would have it, there weren't a lot of examples around her that would help her to date effectively as a professional. She loved numbers, and thought becoming a CPA would be a solid, financially savvy career choice. Once she became a CPA, she worked for a small firm that didn't encourage business development until much later in her career, when she became a partner. In addition, she wasn't provided with a strong mentor, so she learned by observing others when she had time in-between returns. Then, BAM! She found herself a partner, where she was not only compensated on the hours she works and actually got paid for, a.k.a. her "realization rate," she also was told to "go out and get business." Melanie's fellow partners were too busy getting their own business and doing returns and audits themselves — not exactly strong examples of how to generate business. There's one partner who's a "people person" and he's relied upon by the firm to drum up as much business as possible for the other partners. Basically, he's the guy who carries the entire firm, including Melanie.

Now, on the other hand, let's take Duke Frankel as an example. Duke was born into a politically connected family that split its time between Dallas, D.C. and Los Angeles. His father is an attorney, and his mom retired after serving as a three decade Congresswoman. In addition, his grandfather sat at the right hand of a former President. In Duke's case, he had plenty of amazingly effective examples of business dating, including how to initiate conversations and connections, deepen relationships, and maximize results, all with people he considers great friends. Once he graduated from law school (with honors), his dad was able to make several introductions that were instrumental in him finding the perfect opportunity to begin his practice.

Duke had models for how to business date, and Melanie didn't. Does that mean Duke will win the race? For the time being, but don't count Melanie and the Melanies of the world out quite yet {especially if you're one of them!}. I believe business dating can and should be learned. Melanie and Duke will serve as a greater example for you to follow throughout this book.

Business Dating done well is networking on steroids. Skilled networkers are true rainmakers with fantastic relationships that stand the test of time and yield amazing results; all while making it look easy. If you're still reading, I have the sneaky suspicion you would like to be much better at business dating.

Right here at the beginning, I'm going to set some expectations around what you can achieve in your networking pursuits. You must enter into business dating with positive expectations, while at the same time understanding the realities.

The four cornerstones of a long and successful networking career include:

- **Time**: It will take a fair amount of time to find the right people to be your clients and strategic partners. Be prepared to have a lot of bad and so-so business dates as you sort through the vast numbers of professionals on your path to finding the gems.
- **Money**: You will invest a fair amount of money on coffee, lunches, gifts, and potentially, referral fees as you build your stable of solid clients and contacts.
- **Emotion**: You must have a genuine affection and caring for those with whom you engage in a business relationship. Be prepared to put your heart into your relationships.
- **Patience**. To end up on the profitable side of networking, you must view your pursuit as an Ironman Triathlon as opposed to a 100-meter sprint.

Why make the effort? Why should you invest your time, emotion, hard-earned money, and patience into meeting the right people and developing deep, meaningful relationships? Oh, my friend, because the really "good stuff" – and don't you want the good stuff? – is waiting for you on the other side! The long-term benefit to you is an abundance of prosperity, great relationships, happy clients, and true fulfillment. Not necessarily in that order, but when you have all of them in spades, you won't care so much about the order they are in, or the amounts you have.

BUSINESS DATING

The best business relationships are with people you know, like, and trust. They are true win-win relationships in which you feel like you can be authentically yourself, can ask for what you need, give what they need, and both parties are thrilled.

Do these types of relationships sound like the ones you want to develop, starting now and throughout the course of your career? Fabulous ... then let's continue.

Chapter Two:
Why Are You Business Dating?

You meet new people almost every single day. In fact, you probably don't have a "meeting people" problem; you most likely have a "sorting through the people you meet to find the best people" problem. In addition, if you've got some BHAG's {Big, Hairy, Audacious Goals}, you're on the clock and in a hurry. I hear you.

While it is relatively simple and easy to meet new people to add to your network, and therefore making a leap onto what I call the "Trust Bridge" an almost daily occurrence, having the skills and stamina to reach the other side is not for the weak at heart. The goal is to go from one side of the Trust Bridge, the "Nice to meet you" side to the other side, the "I'm so glad, for many reasons, that we've met so I feel comfortable hiring you and/or referring you" side, in the right amount of time, for both parties, for the good of all concerned.

"But Honorée," you might be thinking, *"you've spent a lot of time getting me to this point and what I really want to know is how to have these magical relationships you speak about."* Fair enough. But you can't build the third floor of your residence before you lay the foundation.

A mutually beneficial, long-lasting business or personal relationship is defined as: "a relationship that is advantageous for both parties." In fact, both parties should feel like *they* are getting the better end of the deal. Before I dive into how-to, I'm going to give you a real-life example.

> *Deep relationships are the glue*
> *that hold the world together.*

I first connected with Hal Elrod, author of *The Miracle Morning*, after I posted a review of his book on Goodreads.com, which is an on-line hangout for serious readers and, of course, authors.

To share some valuable back-story, I had been thinking, even prior to reading his book, about what I really wanted as an author. Of course every author wants readers, lots and lots of readers, and I'm no exception. One way to get new readers is to have happy readers give a good or great {preferably 5-star} review on Amazon and Goodreads.com. So, I made it a point to give a great review to each and every book that I thought deserved it.

Within a few days, Hal had contacted me and was interested in discussing adding an additional book to *The Successful Single Mom* book series. Very soon, we partnered to turn *The Miracle Morning* into *The Miracle Morning Book Series*. Out of my desire to give came several amazing things: my friendship with Hal, our business relationship, and more than a dozen other really cool connections and opportunities.

What Hal did really well, and one of the reasons we are working together to this day, is he asked the question, *"How can I add value to you?"* right away. I love that question, and so should you.

What I later learned is that Hal is focused on how he can add value first, instead of trying to figure out what he can get from a relationship. What he wants from his relationships actually stems from what he can give to a relationship. Kinda cool, right?

As an aside, I believe you can add the most value when you've taken the right amount of time, and given the right amount of attention, to those you want to engage in a long-term relationship.

Before you can add people to your network, the first question to ask yourself is, "What do I want from business dating?" If you've read my book *Vision to Reality*, then you probably have not only a long-term vision, but a 100-day vision as well. Simply put, if you don't know what you want, it will be hard for you to know who you need to know. However, once you define what you want, it is easy to delineate who you need to add to your life, business, and circle of influence to more easily and effortlessly reach your goals.

Then, you can take the deliberate and intentional action steps to develop the relationships that matter.

You'll notice I first asked myself what I wanted more of, and then I got busy trying to give that same gift to someone else. You might also notice I had really cool opportunities pop up because of it. At its essence, that's what successful *Business Dating* is all about!

You will want to get *very clear* about the direction of your business and your life before you begin to execute the art of business dating. At the very least, define how much longer you want to be working, and what you want from all that effort.

A few things to consider:

- *How many years do I have left to work?*
- *What is my exit strategy?* Your options include living on retirement income and investments, the sale of your business, living off of royalties, or other leveraged income.
- *How much will I need to live on and how far do I have to go to have that much available to me when I retire, quit working, or change my level of intensity with regard to my work?*

The answers to those questions will inform how assertive and time-aware you need to be in your quest to build a network that will support your desired outcomes. If you're in your twenties, you obviously have much more time to accumulate wealth. If you're in your sixties, your plan of action will be much different.

Once you have clarity, you will be able to set your intentions, determine your direction, sort through everyone you meet to find who you really need to know like a freakin' rock star!

One Night Stand or Life-long Relationship?

Now that you know what you want and have the basic idea of who you need to know (which I will cover in-depth in a upcoming chapter), you'll want to gain even more clarity around your approach to business dating. In other words, you're going to need to buy in to my program and embrace developing mutually beneficial, long-term relationships.

I'll point out the obvious, and something you might have already been thinking: I know plenty of jerks that view their relationships strictly as transactions, and they do quite well for themselves.

You're not wrong. You do know people who are transactional only, in business for what and how much they can get as quickly as possible, and they do seem to do pretty well for themselves. I'm of the opinion they work a *lot* (lot!) harder over the long-term than those who position themselves in cooperative relationships for the right reasons. In the long run, I'd say they have higher client acquisition costs, spend more time at an innumerable number of uninteresting networking events, and are far less fulfilled than they could be.

Ultimately, the type of networking you engage in will determine whether you get some short-term cash today or enjoy long-term riches. In other words, do you want a one-night stand or a life-long relationship?

Perhaps you're not entirely sure. Okay, fair enough. I'm willing to make my case here. Let's explore the benefits and advantages of long-term business relationships.

Let's Talk Cash, Contribution, Connection, and Other Currency

We're talking business dating, emphasis on business, and business is about making money. You get to choose the outcome you desire for each business relationship: make lots of repeat and referral revenue over the long term, or generate some short-term and one-time quick cash.

Arguably, one of the biggest and best benefits of long-term business relationships is the revenue you will be able to generate because of those relationships. Without a doubt, the longer and better someone knows you, the more likely they are to hire you and refer you. You can take your relationships, literally, to the bank.

The longer you've been in a relationship with a strategic partner or client, the higher you perform and the more authentic you are, the more business will come your way – both from that original connection and through them as they refer you. As you increase someone's comfort level with you, they will feel comfortable increasing the amount of business they are willing to extend and refer to you. Many times I have started with just one client at a company, and as time passed, I would add another, and then another.

Another advantage of enduring relationships is the level of trust that eventually occurs between you and your connections. Once you have gotten to know someone really well, you will come to understand, and effectively utilize his or her areas of genius. Because of your knowledge of their strengths, and the trust that exists between you, you know they will take excellent care of you and anyone you send their way.

One of the major driving forces behind my work is my contribution; I want to know I'm making a difference with every coaching session, conversation, presentation, and chapter. Most of the people I'm connected to also focused intently on the positive impact they are able to make with their work. From the divorce attorneys who live to help people traverse one of the toughest times of their lives, to the financial advisors who love to help people create the best plan to help their clients' money grow, to the moving company who loves to help your move be less stressful and "the best move you'll ever make," one thing is for sure, business isn't just about the money.

In short, sustaining relationships have countless benefits including repeat business, making a difference, unending referrals, and even the friendships that result.

So, is it worth it to make the time, effort and monetary investment it takes to develop a measureable number of long-term relationships? I still say *yes*. My position, I hope by now, is clear. I'm a strong advocate for developing deep, meaningful relationships that bear fruit for years to come. Hopefully by now you are firmly planted in my camp and believe long-term relationship building is the way to go.

Let's explore how business dating is similar to, and different from, traditional relationship dating, and what that means for you and your career.

Relationship dating generally has an outcome; you're dating to achieve one of several desired objectives: to find someone to hang out with for a reason, a season, or a lifetime. You may want to get your needs met. You may want to find someone to hang out with, someone who has mutual hobbies and interests while you're building your career, but without marriage in mind. Or, perhaps you want to find your soul mate, your special someone, *the one*.

Business dating is very similar, with some exceptions. Your outcome is to identify those individuals with whom you have mutual interests, knowledge, and especially prospective clients. In business, monogamy is usually not expected or even implied. You can "date" as many other professionals as you'd like. In fact, I suggest that you do (more on that later).

You might be wondering how to effectively pursue and develop relationships in business, while simultaneously wondering where your efforts might be ineffective. Indeed, there are a number of things I see people doing in vain that prevent them from helping as many people as they'd like to help, connecting with as many people as they'd like to connect with, and making as much money as they'd like to make. You might be doing some of these dreadful dating techniques, and not necessarily from a place of malice, more from lack of awareness.

Ineffective Business Dating

The difference between a successful networker and an unsuccessful networker is sometimes inches as opposed to miles. To be fair, what we're taught to do or observe someone else doing, and what actually works are not always the same thing. In fact, very often they are diametrically opposed.

Here are some of the ineffective business dating tactics I've witnessed first-hand:

- *Meeting for the first time and expecting instant gratification.* This is the "one night stand" of business dating. Most likely you won't get hired or receive the best introductions during or immediately following the first meeting {unless that first meeting is truly magical}.
- *Lack of systematic and intentional follow-up.* Just "one touch" is not all it takes, and the first meeting is just the first meeting.
- *Going wide instead of deep.* Yes, you need to meet lots and lots of people. However, it's not just who you know, it's how well you know them. And, quality wins over quantity every single time.
- *Lack of reliability or follow-through; not keeping their word.* There's a saying, "As you pray, move your feet." I say, "As you promise, follow through." In other words, your word is your brand and your word must be sterling.

- *Absence of caring.* Stop saying, "I want to get to know you better" and actually get to know me better. Invite your contacts to lunch, coffee, and events *over and over and over*.

- *Asking too soon.* I know, this sounds a lot like the first bullet. But seriously, asking, "Who do you know that I need to know" before you've known someone more than an hour is too much!

How then, you might be asking, does one "business date" effectively? Great question! For most of the remainder of this book I will address the specific steps you can take to find and develop deep, meaningful relationships with the right people to help you grow your business. But first, we're going to explore the journey you get to take every time you meet someone new. Let's dive right in.

Chapter Three:
The Art of Business Dating

Just like personal relationships, the best business relationships are fun. Both people involved in the relationship enjoy helping each other find new clients, and go out of their way to find clients. Why? Because they are *friends*... they've developed a relationship with someone they now know, like very much, and trust. They have crossed The Trust Bridge.

Your Journey Along the Trust Bridge

Let me clarify using the word *friend*. Just because I have met someone once or twice doesn't mean we're actual friends. We're more "friendly" at this stage, although I may have an inkling of what might grow out of our connection over time. When you first meet someone, you sit at the foot of what I call the Trust Bridge. The first handshake or phone conversation is just the beginning of a journey to the other side of the Bridge, where the fruits of the effort of building a relationship live.

What are the fruits, you ask? Not so fast, sparky! (Have I taught you nothing so far?!) I have to begin by teaching you the stages of an effectively built relationship, where the stages exist on the Trust Bridge, and how long you may sit in each stage. Then and only then, can you discover the potential fruits of each relationship you initiate.

Relationship Stages

There are five stages of a relationship, and each one builds upon the one before it. While every relationship is different, each contains each of the stages. No matter how quickly you progress through each stage, and even if you quickly progress seemingly all the way, each one exists without question.

As I mentioned, when you are just meeting someone for the first time, you aren't even on the Trust Bridge yet. You've barely opened your dialogue, and gotten an inkling of the possibility. You'll see, as you navigate the Stages, how you can safely and successfully access, and cross, the Trust Bridge.

THE INTRODUCTION

Stage One: "Nice to meet you." The initial connection is similar to meeting with someone through a blind introduction, at a coffee shop, or an online dating site.

Read: I don't know you; I don't know if I like you yet or not; and I'm certainly not handing over my money or any of my contacts. You've entered this stage the minute you shake hands with someone, take their first call, or are introduced to them in any way.

The bad news: You may have a very long way to go before you can expect to monetize this relationship.

The great news: The possibilities are endless.

Stage Two: "I'm getting to know you." Also known as: I think we are going to go on a date.

During this stage, your job is to ask great questions, be authentic, and find common interests and even people you both know. Be positive, inquisitive and add value in any way you can.

The bad news: You still have a long way to go.

The great news: You're potentially making positive progress.

GOING FROM KNOW TO LIKE

Stage Three: "I think I like you." In personal relationships, you can spend years in Stage Three. In business dating, you can experience a faster positive result ... but don't bank on it quite yet!

You'll know you entered this stage because, during one of your interactions, you'll be able to see the person across from you relax, lean into the conversation, and share what they are thinking. They will convey with you what could happen if you worked together, or they were able to refer someone with your skills to their clients. While you may not yet, now or ever, be *friends*, you are without a doubt friendly towards each other.

The bad news: The relationship could still go either way. Don't lose patience, get antsy, and make a move prematurely. Ask for something too soon, or act too quickly, and you might spook them. Be prepared to spend as long as it takes in this stage.

The great news: You're {still} making progress. Once you've become friendly, you are well on your way to becoming someone they trust.

GETTING TO TRUST

Stage Four: "I'm starting to trust you." You'll know you entered this stage because your connection starts to feel even more relaxed, and your new friend may discuss the terms of hiring you or mention a specific person they are going to introduce you to right away.

The bad news: One wrong move and you're out. During this stage you could assume "you're in" and by becoming too familiar or comfortable, alienate the person you thought was well on their way to becoming a great connection.

The great news: With every call, email or meeting you have, you can be building more and more good will, greater trust, and a deeper relationship.

Stage Five: "I trust you." People who trust you, personally and professionally, are excited to see you, go out of their way to help you, and you can tell they feel warmly toward you because it's written all over their face.

In relationship dating, Stage Five is "we're going steady," "we're exclusive," even "we're engaged!"

The bad news: You've reached the stage where there is, pretty much, no more bad news. Congratulations!

The great news: You have gotten to know your connection well enough that, if you don't have the keys to their kingdom, you will very soon.

The above stages could take literally sixty minutes or less to sail across. HOWEVER! Most likely it will take many, many meetings, conversations, and interactions to cross the Trust

Bridge. This process could take countless weeks, months or even years, remember it's going to take as long as it takes, and that's perfectly acceptable.

A Few Words of Caution

Have you ever seen two people meet, get engaged or married, only to hear a short time later they've divorced under awful circumstances? Perhaps the amount of time they spent in litigation was many times longer than the length of their courtship? Your initial intuitive feelings of, "Oh, *suh-weet*, I've met my perfect partner" could be spot-on. Yet there's nothing wrong with allowing the relationship to gel and mature over a period of time to double-confirm your initial instincts.

Remember: you have in essence embarked upon a triathlon {Ironman in duration}; you're not running a 100-yard dash. Take your time and allow the relationship to grow, deepen, and evolve. When a relationship is right, it is not only right today, it's right years and years from now.

Remember Duke? He started out life with the advantage of having two very well connected parents. He was able to land in the "I trust you" stage with most folks much faster than Melanie. I'm not saying he could waltz into any situation and hit a home run, but pretty close. While Melanie has had to spend much more time in the initial stages, she has been able to successfully build multiple relationships across many disciplines by recognizing she had to be patient while her relationships were developing. Duke had a head start, but both he and Melanie have ended up in the same place: with strong networks that have paid and continue to pay dividends.

The best relationships are built on trust. With it, you have everything, and without it you have nothing.

The Fruits

Now that you are well versed in the Stages, we can discuss the fruits ... meaning, what are the big-time benefits of taking the time to develop a relationship? There are enough benefits they literally could fill their own book, but for the purposes of our conversation about building your business there are two: cash and connection.

CASH

If you're looking for the fastest, most efficient and effective way to take yourself from rags to riches, being a world-class business dater is your ticket. I'm sure you've heard the saying, "It's not what you know, it's who you know." If you think that saying may sound like an old wives' tale or a cliché saying someone came up with randomly, you'd be, umm ... wrong.

On the other side of the trust bridge is your access to other people's purchasing power. Purchasing power that can and will line your pockets, bank account, or mattresses – whatever you've got.

CONNECTION

Another fruit of your labor is the connections you'll make. A relationship fully developed includes almost unlimited access to someone, their friendship, their contacts and connections, and quite possibly all of their business. Case in point: I have people who reach out to me to "pick my brain" and I truly love to help people. However I, like everyone else, have a limited amount of time and an unending to do list. Nonetheless, when a trusted colleague requests that I spend time with someone, they can consider it done. I know the opposite is also true. When I reach out to someone with a request, they almost always honor it.

Bonus Fruit: CONTRIBUTION

An "extra" fruit of your labor will be the contributions you are going to have the opportunity to make to your connections, as well as their connections, charities, families, and friends. People who don't know you very well may shy away from asking you to "bail them out of jail" to raise money for Muscular Dystrophy, and they won't invite you to an annual gala where they've bought a table for $500 a plate. But a solid connection will include you in the important activities that transpire throughout the year, and won't hesitate to participate in your important goings-on. In other words, you will have even more opportunities to make the world a better place than you do today.

Even more good news ...

I didn't exactly reveal *all* of the Relationship Stages. Traversing the Five Stages successfully reveals a possible super-amazing sixth stage: friendship.

BONUS Stage: We're friends ... and this is where relationships really get good. When the stars have aligned, and the parties involved sense a deeper connection, it is extremely possible to develop a true life-long friendship that transcends a traditional work relationship.

When you're lucky enough to discover these gems amongst your network, treat them with all of the reverence and respect you would any relationship of true importance.

Remember: at your first meeting, every amazing outcome is a possibility. Your role is to get on, and stay on, the Trust Bridge until you've gotten to where you desired to go in the first place, or determine the person you're sitting across from isn't your cup of tea. You get to decide because you're in the driver's seat.

Getting on the Trust Bridge is easy as pie, but staying in good standing with your prospects and strategic partners until you've crossed over to the other side requires a strong set of skills. I've written this book because clearly more people need to know the ins and outs of networking effectively. When you're ready to up your game, turn the page.

Chapter Four:
The Don'ts and Do's of Business Dating

There are two main components to successful *Business Dating:*

- What to do, and
- What not to do.

Just as you can take a relationship a long way by doing the right things, you can stop a nicely progressing relationship in it's tracks ... or even end one altogether with the wrong moves. As you are getting to know new connections, and as you deepen established relationships, you want to advance with care.

Because I'm not one to focus on the negative for very long {usually just long enough to figure out how to eliminate it}, let's get the "what not to do's" out of the way.

What Not To Do

As you know, from watching others make networking faux pas and probably some of your own personal experiences, a misstep can spoil even the most promising relationship. My goal here is to take the mystery out of whether or not a particular action is a "do" or a "don't." While intentions may be pure, doing any or all of these in a relationship is sure to take you off track.

Here is a short list of what not to do when you're trying to expand or leverage your network:

1. Attempt to take before you do everything you can to give. Obviously, the goal of networking is to connect with people who can help you make a sale, get a referral, or establish a contact. When we network, we want something.

But at first it's not about asking for what *you* want. Make sure you hear and digest this: at the beginning of a relationship, do not ask for what you want. *Never* ask for what you're looking for in an initial meeting, or even the first few meetings. In fact, you may never ask for what you want, because you might never have to ask (more on that shortly). Forget about what you might be able to get, and focus on what you can *give*.

Note: If they ask how they can help you, you can certainly answer with what you're looking for, or needing, right now. Sometimes the person we meet has the same generous spirit and servant's heart. When you encounter them, it is a blessed day indeed.

2. Assume others should care about your needs. Maybe you're desperate, low on business, or revenue is tight. Maybe partnering with a major player in your industry, or getting that potential client to hire you today, could instantly transform red ink into black. Here's what you need to know: it's not that people don't care, *it's that they don't care*. People really care about themselves and those closest to them, and you're "new," which means they can only really care so much at this point. This is not a harsh reality (I can hear you!); it's just the truth.

Don't expect others to respond to your needs, not yet. People may sympathize but helping you is not their responsibility. In fact, sharing too much too soon can be your one-way ticket to the end of that relationship. The only way to make connections is to care about the needs of others first.

3. Take a shotgun approach. Some people network with reckless abandon, tossing out business cards like confetti, and trying to meet everyone in their path. Networking is and isn't a numbers game. The three-foot rule, which states: *"If someone has a pulse, is breathing and is within 3 feet of you, they are a possible prospect or strategic partner for your business."* is alive and well. It is true you'll need to meet lots and lots of people to find the life-long gems you're searching to find. But there's a way to find them, and it's not necessarily the way you have probably been doing it up to this point. Shortly you'll learn my no-fail way to build a network that rocks your world ... and your bottom line {so hang in there and keep reading!}.

4. Assume tools create connections. You can have the biggest social media following in the world. In fact, Twitter followers, Facebook friends, and LinkedIn connections are all great, *if* you do something with those connections. In all likelihood, your Twitter followers aren't reading your tweets. Your Facebook friends rarely visit your page. Your LinkedIn connections aren't checking your updates.

Tools provide a convenient way to establish connections, and they are an excellent way for someone to verify your expert standing, but to maintain those connections you still have to put in the work. Any tool that is easy or automated won't establish the connections you really need. Social media is just such a tool—use it well, and it can pay dividends. Plan to use social media tools that make your life easier and that ensure you take the right action at the right time.

5. Reach too high. If your company provides financial services, establishing a connection with Warren Buffett would be amazing. You might want a celebrity endorser for your product and Shaq would be perfect! If you need seed capital, meeting up with Mark Cuban and the rest of *Shark Tank* would be awesome. Amazing, perfect, awesome … and nearly impossible.

The best connections are mutually beneficial. What can you offer Buffett, Shaq, or Cuban? Probably not much, right now, or ever. You may desperately want to connect with the "top people," but the right to connect is not based on want or need. You must earn the right to connect, and the right to be heard. Perhaps someday you will earn the right to be top dog, but in the meantime focus on your peers and others at your same level.

6. Presume intimacy. If I've met you once or twice, we are not *good friends*. If you've given me free advice over a cup of coffee, I am not your client. Over-stating a relationship, based on your assumption of the depth and intimacy of that relationship, can work against you at the very least, and really backfire at the very most.

I've been in situations where someone has provided a hot endorsement when they, in fact, have never used my services. I'm certain it was in good faith and with the best of intentions, but the follow-up questions of "What exactly did she help you achieve?"

and "What was the best part of working with her?" required back-pedaling and mild embarrassment. Authentic admiration, and transparency about one's true level of involvement works best in business dating, as well as in every other situation.

Let me say this again: true relationships are built over time. It takes multiple meetings and conversations for a relationship to gel, to solidify, and be one you can rest solidly upon.

7. Keep score. I actually read in a book, "I note who pays each time we meet so I know who is supposed to pay the next time." It takes a lot of energy to remember who paid last time, or exactly how many referrals you have been given in an attempt to keep people in line in your mind or ensure *quid pro quo* is in full force and effect.

My advice is to literally throw out any scorekeeping you've been doing. If you can give someone twenty referrals, give them. As a giver, you will naturally receive the right referrals at the right time. I have a belief, "You can't out give the Universe." I believe in the unseen forces that have my back, so I never hesitate to give whenever and wherever I can. I know my generosity is going to come back in spades, and not always from where it was given. It provides me a free space from which to give, and I recommend adopting the same attitude.

8. Waste people's time. This may sound like number five said another way, and it may be … and yet it really isn't the same concept at all. You must be mindful of what the other person gains by hearing from or meeting with you. There are several ways I observe individuals wasting others' time:

- Giving a lead instead of a referral. The underlying driver of a lead is 'hope' and *hope* is not helpful. I've been given someone's number, told to call and use a person's name, only to have the recipient of my call audibly irritated to have their time wasted. Alternatively, I've been the recipient of unexpected calls {telemarketers, anyone?} that were both interruptions and time-wasters. Not good!

- Asking to "pick their brain" over coffee. This is both rude and disrespectful. Unless you are attempting to establish a bona-fide mentor or client relationship, you must offer to pay for someone's time. They may have a generous spirit and decline payment, especially because you've offered it. But it's up to you to make the offer and be willing to back it up.

Lawyers don't want to give free legal advice. CPAs don't want to give free tax advice. Authors don't want to give free writing and publishing advice. Do you want to give free advice, which is tantamount to wasting your time and ultimately your money? I'm sure you don't, unless special circumstances are involved. Be sure to ask yourself, "What's in it for the person I'm meeting with?" before asking for that very meeting.

Okay, whew! I'm glad that's over! I much prefer to abandon the soapbox and point you in a positive direction. I'm sure you're ready, too! Now for the good, positive part.

People will love you right about the time they know you love them.

What To Do

Every action you take in building a relationship can truly be a fun adventure. Meeting new people, learning about them and discussing how you can add value to their lives, careers, friends and family can be the high point of each day.

Take note, here is what to do in each and every relationship to make it the long-lasting, mutually-beneficial connection you want it to be:

1. Give, give, give. Rinse. Repeat. In every conversation, ask a variation of these questions: "How can I support you?" and "What do you need right now?"

Ask yourself prior to each meeting, "How can I add value to this person?"

Let's suppose we're having lunch today. There is at least one thing you need right now, and wouldn't you like me to give it to you? I'm going to guess what you need would either solve a problem you have or help you reach a goal you're chasing. Well, I have something I need, too, and I would be thrilled if you gave it to me. You would elevate yourself in my eyes, and I would feel compelled to give you what you need right back. I think reciprocity, more than any other business dating technique, is one every person in business needs to master, especially because your platform is built on your personal brand.

Wikipedia explains "Reciprocity" as:

~reciprocity in social psychology refers to responding to a positive action with another positive action, rewarding kind actions.

~as a social construct, reciprocity means that in response to friendly actions, people are

frequently much nicer and much more cooperative than predicted by the self-interest model; conversely, in response to hostile actions they are frequently much more nasty and even brutal – <u>Wikipedia</u>.

In other words, do something nice and people will feel compelled to do something nice for you in return {and, as you can see, the opposite can also be very true}. The way, *the only way,* to incite the Law of Reciprocity, is to be the one who gives first. Find out what the person in front of you needs, and do your best to give it to them.

Remember: you don't have to actually give it to them. You have to think about what they need. You have to try to deliver. Then, let them know you've thought about it, and you've tried. A little effort goes a long way. It matters. It matters a lot. Don't you agree?

Additionally, as I stated previously, sometimes you give and when you receive something back it isn't from the place you gave. Be open to receiving your good from any channel.

2. Care. Care about others first; then, and only then, will they truly care back. Have you heard the saying, "People don't care how much you know until they know how much you care." It's true, true, true.

If you don't actually care about other people, if you're in business for what you can get, for the money you can make and it's all about you, you, you, then stop right now and return this book. We are philosophically not in alignment and continuing to read this book would be a travesty because it would be a colossal waste of your most precious resource: your time. If you care about people, kindly keep reading.

All right, you're still reading. I'm so glad! Back to our hypothetical lunch conversation—you can bet I'm going to ask how you're doing. I'm also going to ask what I can do to help you. I'm asking because I care, I genuinely want to help you, and I could not care less whether you can do anything for me. When you care about someone, genuinely and authentically care about them, you give without expecting something in return. And, it feels so good to give!

"But you just talked about the Law of Reciprocity, Honorée." I can hear you thinking. *"I'm confused. You're contradicting yourself."* No, dear reader, I'm not. I'm telling you to just care about the other person. Give first without expecting something in return. The Law of Reciprocity means they will feel compelled to do the same. That, my friend, is called a win-win. And a win-win is exactly what we're going for here, both today and over the next fifty years.

3. Be intentional and purposeful. The antidote for the shotgun approach is to spend some time in isolation and deep thought, contemplating, deciding, and defining exactly who you need to add to your network and why.

In my executive coaching practice, I have my clients build what I call the 12x12 Matrix: an intentional and purposeful network-building tool that is both directive and non-directive.

At its core, the 12x12 helps you to:

find someone you can help, determine whether they might (someday) be able to help you, and then approach them on your own terms.

The first step is to always select the people you want to network with, based upon your goals and objectives. You ask yourself this question:

- *Where, as in, what discipline or profession, do the majority of my referrals {other than through current clients} come from?*

Identify the eleven disciplines or professions that most frequently refer, or could refer business to you.

Without going too deep quite yet, I'll give a quick example. Certified Public Accountants {CPAs}, who specialize in small business returns, usually receive the most referrals from these three types of professionals: business attorneys, tax attorneys, and financial advisors.

Having this knowledge means CPAs can identify professionals in those specific disciplines. These folks are the most likely to be excellent strategic partners. They can then intentionally and purposefully connect with them.

Alternatively, it wouldn't make much sense for a small-business-centered CPA to seek out fortune 500 CFOs, dog walking professionals, or roofers. Yet, when a CPA goes to a networking event where anyone can attend, without an intended outcome, the latter and/or a mix of people, is most likely who they will encounter.

4. Use tools that help you develop long-term connections. In addition to the 12x12, there are some pretty nifty tools you can use to stay in touch with your budding and developing network. Your email, combined with email marketing through a list-building service such as Aweber or MailChimp, and even social media branding through Twitter,

Facebook, and LinkedIn can not only raise your profile and spread your brand, they can help you stay in touch at the right time.

The 12x12 will direct you to network with exactly who you need to network with, exactly when you need to network with them. You'll get the step-by-step instructions, including links to tools you can download instantly, in the next chapter.

5. Establish mutually beneficial connections. One of your underlying goals is to find people who can benefit from your knowledge and insight, or from your connections. Or both.

The status level of your connections is irrelevant, i.e., they can be older or younger, more or less experienced. All that matters is whether you can help each other reach your goals.

6. Take the time it takes. You've read this before, in this very book: you won't know how long it will take someone to reach their internal level of comfort, and frankly so you can reach your internal level of comfort. You'll need to settle in and be ready to have as many lunches, coffees, meetings, golf tournaments, galas, and shoe shopping adventures as it takes. Once you've identified that someone could possibly be "the one" {one of your ones}, then you keep on keepin' on until you cross the Trust Bridge.

7. Give give give give give. As I said, *"You can't out-give the Universe."* is one of my favorite sayings. You may be more, or less, of a believer in that concept than I am, but we can probably agree on one thing: the more you give, the more you eventually get. I can promote someone's products or services with a smile, an email, or a strong word of endorsement. Not only is it fun to give, it usually costs little or nothing to make such a positive impact.

8. Give bona-fide referrals. This is a big one! One of the fastest ways to a professional contact's heart is through their wallet, and the referral of a pre-qualified prospective client is an excellent way to prove yourself to a worthy contact.

- A lead is a person that *might* have an interest, authority and/or budget in someone's products or services.
- A referral is someone that is excited to talk to the person from whom they can purchase a much-needed product or service.

While a lead is good, a referral is fantastic! You want to give bona-fide referrals as much as possible, and as often as possible.

Make the Connection

I have a three-step process I've developed to pre-qualify, gain permission, and make a connection. I'm sure you want to know what it is, so here you go:

Let's assume you're in a conversation with someone, and you hear a need a strategic partner can fill or determine there's a problem they can solve. Follow these three steps to make a great referral:

1. Ask the person with the need if they'd like to meet someone you know personally who might be able to help them. Explain who they are, how you know them, and how long you've known them.
2. Call the person you believe can help, explain the situation, and make sure you're right! I recently had a previous client "refer" someone to me who was looking to buy a condo in my

area. Since I'm neither a condo owner nor a real estate agent, I was unable to help and it was a waste of time for both of us.

3. Make an introduction. I prefer to send both parties an email with each other's contact information and let them communicate amongst themselves. It's always a great idea to ask each person their preferred method of communication for introductions.

The Introduction

When I've gotten the go-ahead from both parties to proceed with an introduction, I send an email similar to this:

SUBJECT: INTRODUCTION

John & Bill,

Meet each other!

John, Bill Smith is a top-shelf corporate attorney with eighteen years of experience. He helps companies from formation to liquidation, as well as having a hand in many mergers and acquisitions. You can read about him here {link to bio on website}. You can connect with him via email, above, or at 555-555-5555.

Bill, John Davis is a family attorney with more than a dozen years helping wealthy clients navigate the challenges of divorce, child custody, and modification agreements. Read about him here {link to bio}. He has a need to strike out on his own, and could use your expertise in business formation. Connect with him via email, above, or at 555-555-5555.

Gentlemen: I feel it would be beneficial for the two of you to connect as there seems to be a need that could be filled immediately, as well as future mutual synergies. I look forward to hearing you've successfully connected. Let me know how else I can be of service to you.

To your success!
Honorée

Getting "permission" to make a connection from both parties is helpful, but in lieu of a conversation with the person to whom you're making the referral, let common sense be your guide. Your strategic partners may not want everyone to have the level of access to them you have earned over time. I advise you to ask before you share someone's personal cell phone number or private email address. Unless I know that's okay, I give the main or direct office number along with an email.

You now have guiding tools for networking. It's time to add some structure to your knowledge. Knowledge is only powerful when it's put into action, so let's get into action!

Chapter Five:
The Structure Sets You Free

It's time to make your networking work, and to do that you will need to step up your levels of intention, intensity, and purpose, so you will finally get the results you're after.

Adding intention, intensity, and purpose to your networking efforts means you won't have to wait months or years to see the results of the network you've built. I'm sure you've met seasoned professionals who, after thirty years, know everyone they need to know, and combined with their knowledge and experience are held with high respect due to their professional results and, of course, the wealth they've accumulated.

I'm sure you'd like to have their results without having to wait several decades. I mean come on, we live in an instant download "I-want-it-now" time in history, and I'm sure you would like some now-rather-than-later results. {I know, me too!}

That's why I'm going to peel back the layers of my network building system, so you know what to do, when to do it, and with exactly the right people. Starting right now.

The 12x12 System™

The 12x12 System™ was born out of my desire to do two things: effectively keep track of my contacts, and to stop missing opportunities.

I have always been pretty good about staying on top of my networking efforts, but as a visual person, using a database wasn't as effective for me as having a visual tool I could use on a daily basis. One I could look at and instantly know who was in my network, when our last connection took place, and when I should follow up to "keep the love alive."

The original 12x12 Matrix™ wasn't an expertly organized Excel document with identified columns of targeted professionals and notes inserted with crucial information. No, at the beginning it was a poster board with 3x3 Post-it Sticky Notes on the wall of my office. I hadn't mastered the System quite yet {it wasn't even a true System when I first started!}, but being able to see the names of the people I was building strategic partner relationships with was critical to keeping me on track and focused.

The 12x12 System™ in its current and time-tested form is your guide to business networking gold. This step-by-step process will help you to create a viable and enviable network, even if you have never networked before, are new to your profession, or are shy or hesitant about networking. Or all of the above.

Until now, you have most likely been networking in a haphazard and disorganized manner. As professionals, we've been taught to "go to networking events" and "meet as many people as possible" in order to achieve our goals, meet our numbers, and earn more this year than last year. Unintentional networking creates random and hit-or-miss results.

You have probably met excellent prospects and incredible professionals along your networking journey, along with lots and lots of people that were, frankly, a colossal waste of your time.

In fact, going to an event, any event, is better than doing nothing. Honestly, though, it's not that much better. It's time to stop randomly networking and finally get strategic and intentional about your networking. It's time to do the actions that get the results you desire.

Utilizing the 12x12 System™ is easy, fun, efficient and effective (four of my favorite things). The System takes the guesswork out of networking as a whole, and it also is a directed method for exactly what to do on a micro-level. Follow the System and you will always know what to do *today* to expand your network and "business date" effectively today and hereafter.

The Four Phases of the 12x12 System™

There are four phases in the System, and each builds upon the next: **Identify, Organize, Discover,** and **Connect**.

Identify

First and foremost, you will identify the professional categories most likely to refer you business.

Organize

Next, you will organize the contacts you already have within the Matrix.

Discover

Organizing will reveal the key people you already know, and help you discover the "holes" that exist in your network.

Connect

You now can start to connect with the right Strategic Partners and Centers of Influence in an organized, intentional and purposeful way.

Step One: Identify

Let's start with your first step. Remember back in Chapter 2 when I referenced getting clear about your outcomes before you started networking? Your very next step is to ask yourself some questions, and this will direct your networking actions from this point forward.

Before you leave your office to go to even one more coffee or general membership meeting, you need to know who you're going to meet with, and exactly why you're meeting with them {both for yourself and them}.

Question 1: Where does most of my business come from?

More than likely, your new business comes from either referrals of existing clients, and from other professionals (your actual or probable strategic partners) who also serve those who fit into your ideal client profile.

Oh sure, you'll have the occasional inbound call that results in new business or meet a random stranger who turns out to be a perfect fit in a coffee shop. I've experienced both scenarios, and getting that type of business is awesome ... and although it happens, you won't be able to count on it happening enough to reach and exceed your goals.

Question 2: What are the logical and most likely professional categories and/or sources that send or can send new business to me? In other words, "Who are the professionals that serve my target clients that don't compete with me?"

There are professionals who serve your ideal clients and are not in any way in competition with you. There are professionals who serve your ideal clients who provide similar but not the same products and/or services. In any profession, there are complementary disciplines and *these are the people you need to know.*

For example, if you are a financial advisor, you need to know:

- CPAs
- Tax Attorneys
- Business Attorneys
- Insurance providers
- Business Brokers
- Estate Planning Attorneys
- Divorce/Family Attorneys
- Mortgage Brokers
- Residential Real Estate Agents
- Commercial Real Estate Agents
- Bankers
- Human Resource Managers
- Business Coaches

While the majority of my work has been with service professionals, the 12x12 System of Business Dating works with any profession.

For example, if you are an interior designer, you'll want to connect with:

- Furniture stores
- Accessory stores
- Painters
- Real Estate Agents
- Home staging companies
- Home Builders
- Handymen
- Moving Companies
- Flooring Companies
- Home Inspectors
- Home Insurance Providers
- Cabinet Finishers
- Pool Companies
- Landscape Architects
- Home Theater Consultants
- Plumbers

Coach's Action: Before you continue, download your complimentary 12x12 Matrix at **HonoreeCorder.com/Resources**. Next, fill in eleven of your categories using the instructions that follow.

The How-to: you'll put the *most likely* category in the left-most column. From left to right, go from *most likely* to *least likely* with the identified strategic partner professions. From top to bottom, you'll put the *most likely* individuals in the top boxes, graduating to *least likely*.

In other words, in general CPAs are *most likely* to receive referral business from business attorneys, tax attorneys and financial advisors, so these three professions will occupy the three left-most columns. The three professions they are *least likely* (but still likely!) to receive business from are insurance providers and real estate agents, so these two profession will occupy the boxes on the right-hand side of the Matrix.

The 12th category is *miscellaneous*. This is where you'll put in key and effective centers of influence {the people you know who know everyone} that don't necessarily have their own categories. These can include business and executive coaches, recruiters and headhunters, consultants, or any other ancillary professional that is well networked, connected and can potentially be helpful {and vice-versa}.

The order in which the categories are placed informs and directs your networking efforts. Some categories will provide many more referrals than others, some will provide less, and some won't provide very many at all. But all of your identified categories hold at least some promise and you want to cover all of your bases and become "the best networked person in town." Right? Right!

Coach's Note: Your 12x12 Matrix is a living document. My two pieces of advice for you are: {1} go with your gut and {2} don't overanalyze. You will create, revise, and continue to revise over time. There are no right or wrong answers. No matter what, your actions now far exceed and trump anything you've been doing up to this point!

Step Two: Organize

Once you've identified your complementary professional categories, fill in the names of the people you already know.

Put only the connections you have that make sense, i.e., they have a solid network, are well connected, fit into a category (or could be placed in the *Other* category). Most importantly, make sure you like them and they like you.

Coach's Action: You probably have more contacts than you think. Go through your phone, that drawer full of business cards you haven't touched in awhile, and your LinkedIn contacts. Refer to current and previous client lists. Think about who you know from BNI {Business Networking International}, Rotary Club, church, Bible study, Toastmasters, the Chamber of Commerce, and any other networking or interest group you've visited or belong to.

Step Three: Discover

You have some boxes filled in – congratulations! You probably have between thirty-five and eighty contacts that actually qualify to be on your 12x12 Matrix. I've seen everything from *three* to over 300. In both cases, my clients didn't have the business they wanted, not even close. Being heavily networked and being effectively networked is not the same thing.

Don't have a panic attack if you only have a handful of boxes filled. One attorney was shocked to realize that after seven years of practice and six months into starting his own firm, he could only identify a half-dozen (yes, out of 144 possibles) professionals that *might* be a good fit for his 12x12 Matrix.

Don't worry kids, he did over $150,000 in billable hours last *month*, after just two years of working the 12x12 System.

You might realize you've got one heck of a network already built, and if so, right on! Whether you have three people or 103, this is just the beginning. Chances are, there is so much low hanging fruit in your 12x12 Matrix. Things are about to get exciting!

Coach's Action: From top to bottom, organize your contacts in each column from *most likely* to *least likely* to send you business.

The easiest way to rank them is by the business they've already sent. If they haven't relayed business quite yet, but you've now identified them as someone who could and should be sending you business, use your best guess. The least likely person to send you business is still likely to refer and they may just send the perfect person right when you can help them the most.

Step Four: Connect

You've guessed it, ladies and gentlemen. This is the actual Business Dating part of our program. Once you've filled in your boxes, you can start actually reaching out and meeting with people.

Let the fun begin!

<u>Chapter Six</u>:
Getting to Know You …
Getting to Know All About You &
{I Think} I Like You

I recently attended a luncheon where I met a pair of professionals. They understood the depth of my network because the host made several references to it, and seemed interested in meeting with me, they said, to determine if there were any mutual synergies. Since I have worked in a myriad of professional disciplines as an executive coach, including with those in the same profession as these individuals, and have clients and connections that could be both strategic partners and clients for them, I was interested in meeting with them as well.

This meeting, however, became a case study outlining an ineffective "first date," i.e., our first meeting turned out to be a disaster.

The Bad Business Date

Upon my arrival, after a short speech about how our meeting was meant to be about "developing our relationship," I was immediately subjected to rapid-fire questions about my past experience and who specifically was in my network. I could handle it, but it was a bit uncomfortable.

In my work, as I'm sure in yours, discretion is key. Without any discovery conversation, I was asked who they might know that was a client. When I refused to share the specific names of individuals (at my clients' requests), I was told my secrecy was "weird." Still uncomfortable, the meeting became downright awkward.

Because their company provided an in-house coach, they let me know in no uncertain terms they would *not* be hiring me, but perhaps they could make introductions to their clients. Okay, fair enough.

The over-confident duo also shared that they were *different* than every other person in their industry; they performed their expertise in a way that no other person was able to do (even as they sat surrounded by the offices of people *just like them*). Additionally, they said that they, unlike all of the others, *actually cared about their clients.* What? Professionals that care about their clients? Shut up! Wait … were they insinuating that all of the other people in their industry didn't care at all about their clients? Hmmm.

The closing clincher was that upon reviewing my connections on LinkedIn, they had prepared a suggested list of people they would like me to introduce to them.

Okay, given I barely know you, I'm certainly not going to make introductions, *especially* because this hasn't been {like some other first dates I've had}, a situation where I've felt like I've met a long-lost best friend. Quite the opposite, in fact! I couldn't wait to leave and felt resentful I had wasted two hours of my life I couldn't get back.

Have you ever felt the same way in an initial business meeting? For those of you that have, I bet you'd like to never feel that way again! {Me, too!}

Upon reflection, I'm going to rank this meeting in the top three worst "first business dates" I've ever had. There is a silver lining: everyone gets to benefit from how I spent that time!

As a coach, I don't think of things so much as "good or bad" or "right or wrong," I'm more interested in whether something is "effective or ineffective." This first meeting, my friends, was completely ineffective.

I'm sure the two people I met with are perfectly nice people with good intentions. They were, while an extreme example, representative of professionals out in the marketplace every single day, who are ineffective at building their networks and wondering why they aren't getting the traction they want in their businesses.

The Trust Bridge

By this point, you now know who you need to network with, how to navigate some of the intricacies of each and every relationship, how to keep it moving in the right direction, and how to avoid inadvertently tanking the relationship before it's had a chance to mature.

Breaking news: You've now stepped squarely onto the Trust Bridge. To get to the other side, where the cash, contribution and other currency lives ... and you're just itching to get to, requires the focus, tenacity, patience, and determination of a small child who wants a cookie. And I mean, this kid *really, really* wants that cookie.

In short, you are now *business dating.* I'm sure you still have some unanswered questions about how exactly to deepen each relationship so you become the top of mind strategic partner of choice for each and every person you're dating.

While it might not be possible to be the first choice for every single strategic partner, you only need a handful of folks that truly think you were the one who hung the moon to have a growing and profitable business year over year.

In my executive and business coaching practice, my clients each develop their own 12x12 Matrix. They are excited to have a directed process to help them expand their relationships and networks intentionally. To a person, there are two questions they ask most often:

- **Question #1**: How often should I get in touch with my strategic partners?
- **Question #2**: What in the world do I say when I call and/or meet with them?

Those are terrific questions, and you're in luck! I can answer them for you.

Question #1: How often should I get in touch with my strategic partners?

Answer #1: Once you've had an initial meeting, you determine whether the professional you've met with is:

- A prospective client.
- A prospective strategic partner.
- A potential friend.
- All of the above.

- None of the above.

Prospective client: Surprise! You sit in front of a professional who holds a spot on your 12x12 Matrix. As you're describing the products or services you offer, they say, "I need that for myself!" *Total bonus!* This person is now a prospective client and you'll follow up with them just as you would any other prospective client. I'll touch on my strategies for effective prospective client follow-up in Chapter 8.

Prospective strategic partner: This key category is where most of the professionals you encounter will fall, and therefore, this is where you'll focus most of your time and attention: on them and their network.

Potential friend: When the sun, moon and stars align, you may find yourself in the most amazing place of all: identifying someone with whom you can share a friendship that extends beyond the professional relationship.

All of the above: This is the mother lode, folks, the trifecta of awesomeness: a client, strategic partner, *and* friend. They don't come along very often, but when they do, consider yourself a pretty lucky person.

None of the above: And then there's *this*. You meet with someone once, or even a few times, only to determine they aren't your cup of tea. You discover their values, goals or even political leanings are diametrically opposed to your own. There's good news even here: as of 2013, the population of planet Earth is 7.13 billion people. So when you meet someone you don't particularly care for, it's quite all right. Keep sorting through the people you meet until you find the people you're looking to find.

How to Nurture Your Strategic Partners

As I have mentioned previously, you're going to spend the lion's share of your time developing and nurturing strategic partners. The trickiest part of follow up can be the *how often* piece, meaning when you put someone into your 12x12 System and you don't pre-determine when the next time is that you need to follow up, you could sit and stare at their name for months or even years without taking action.

Inaction is akin to death rattle. Inaction breeds doubt and fear, causes a lack of self-confidence and most importantly, eliminates any possibility of success. You will note this is the exact opposite of our intended outcome: success. Failure doesn't feel good, and I want you to feel great! So keep reading.

The last thing you want to do is identify a solid potential strategic partner, and then miss all of the great things that can come from that relationship *because you fail to stay in touch.* I'm sure you can think of a time you missed an opportunity by "this much" because the business or sale went to another professional *just like you* because the referring person or actual client couldn't lay their hands on your information or remember your name at just the moment they needed you.

The first hurdle you must get over is the habit you have of procrastinating. If you've been listening to the voice in your head that says, "Well, they know what I do, if they need me they'll call," or worse, "I don't want to bother them," it's time to get over it and get on with it.

Stay in Touch Like Your Life Depends On It ... Because it Does!

I've got some incredibly good news for you: the actions you will want to take aren't complicated or expensive. They don't take a ton of time, aren't expensive, and you don't have to be a genius to do them.

What you will want to do is determine, based on your initial conversations, how often you'll want to be in touch. As part of the 12x12 System, there are guidelines for follow up, and here they are:

If after your initial discussion {or two} you determine: {a} you like them *and* {b} they like you *and* {c} they have the exact same target client you do, you'll want to follow up with them every month or every other month. You will assign them a "1" for every month, or "2" for every other month, on your 12x12 Matrix, and schedule them for follow-up in the chosen time frame. And then you'll actually follow-up with them. For real. Trust me when I say intentional, consistent follow-up works like a charm.

Perhaps your target clients have similar qualities, but they aren't exactly the same, you'll want to get in touch with them about every three to four months. You will assign them a "3" for every three months, or "4" for every four months on your 12x12 Matrix, and schedule them for follow-up in the chosen time frame.

If you have similar target clients, but for some reason you don't quite hit it off, you don't want to close the door entirely, but they certainly don't need a ton of your time and attention. Give them a "6" for an every six month follow up, and plan to follow up with them every six months.

Said very simply, you'll follow up with each occupant of your 12x12 Matrix two, three, four, six, or twelve times each year. There's no hard and fast rule and some people will become "1s" and "2s" that started out as a "6," and vice versa.

What you want to avoid is waiting too long in between follow-ups. Waiting too long may cause them to hire or refer someone else, or even lose the initial enthusiasm they had at your first meeting.

For those of you worried about following-up too often, well, let's just say from what I've seen over the years, there are *very few people who follow-up too often.* If you're worried about it, you're probably not one of them.

Who Does the Following Up?

The short answer: *you.* But first, let me explain with some background about personal dating, and how the masculine and feminine roles factor in to business.

In personal relationships, the masculine energy is the hunter, and the feminine energy is the hunted. The masculine role pursues the feminine, while the feminine waits and hope. I'm generalizing a bit, so bear with me. Everyone has the ability to access masculine and feminine energy and these "roles" are not designated to which gender you were born.

To my happily married male readers, you will recognize yourself as the person who identified the woman you wanted to be your wife and you set out on a mission to make it so. Even if, up to this point, you haven't found someone you want to marry, you without question have pursued a relationship with intention and purpose.

Ladies, our traditional role is to sit back and wait for someone to pursue us. We provide an environment that allows us to be approached, and send signals that let our pursuers know they are on the right track.

In personal relationships, the masculine and feminine roles are not only customary; it is how we're wired biologically *from the days of the caveman.*

In business to be most effective, everyone must take the masculine role. Regardless of whether you're a man or a woman, once you have determined someone is meant to be a strategic partner or even a client, you must take ownership of the relationship. Regardless of your gender, you must access our hunter. You will control the direction and timing of each relationship and pursue it from the perspective of someone who has an outcome in mind, and you're making that outcome a reality. I outline this concept further, including specific action steps, later in this chapter.

Who Occupies The 12x12 Matrix?

Everyone you generally like, who could potentially send you business, and vice versa, should occupy a spot on your 12x12 Matrix ... unless, and until, "someone better" comes along. Now, don't think I'm a hater or an elitist, because I'm neither. But I know from experience some people love me, some people like me, and some people don't resonate with me at all. The reverse is true as well. However, I would rather have someone to refer to my clients and connections, as needed than have no one at all. As you meet more and more people, you'll find yourself gravitating toward those you like more than others {there's absolutely nothing wrong with this!}, and letting others fall away.

The longer you work to build your network, the more people you will have on your 12x12 Matrix that you love and adore and would refer in a New York minute, and very few people that are on there because you want to have all of your boxes filled. In the case of your 12x12 Matrix, quality wins over quantity, and yet it's always good to have a number of people you know. This allows you to be of service to just about everyone, and usually right in the nick of time.

Coach's Tip: Just because you don't love someone, doesn't mean the person you refer to them won't think they are the best thing since sliced bread. Make the introductions you think might work, and some will work out beautifully.

A Few Words about "Scheduling for Follow-up"

Lest you get stuck on how you might "schedule them for follow-up in the chosen time frame," I'm going to address that right now, and with brief, effective strategies you can implement immediately. You have a couple of options, and my advice is to keep it simple. So, choose from one of the following:

1. Use the client management system provided to you by your company. ACT! is a popular option and it will work for you just fine. If you have a system or a process that works for you, then work it.
2. You can use my 'system,' which consists of using your email system's calendaring option. Very simply, I schedule each person for 8 a.m. on the date that makes sense for follow-up. My contacts automatically pop up at 8 am on the day I'm meant to check in with them.

Example: If I've decided our next conversation should take place in about three months, I'm going to put you on a date that makes sense three months from now. That morning I'll get a reminder we have an "appointment" and I'll get in touch with you that day.

Are you good so far, and feeling better about setting up your next business date, as well as keeping track of all of your contacts? Good. Let's keep going.

Question #2: What in the world do I say and do when I call and/or meet with them?

Answer #2: Oh, yes, the awkward "I don't know what to say" next step. This whole book is about business dating, and dating, at its very core, is about getting to know the other person better than you know them in the beginning. Your sole focus is to get to know the person on the other end of the line or side of the table as well as you possibly can, so that you can do two things:

- Send them the business they are looking to find.
- Introduce them to the clients and connections you know who need their services.

Yes, that's right, you're putting yourself right smack in the middle of a business love connection. You're making business happen and money change hands. You are the hero of this program, the person who is making not one, not two, but *three* people {at least!} very, very happy.

But we are not taught, as professionals and networkers, to do anything more than have one, maybe two, initial contacts or meetings. We meet, exchange cards and cursory information, and then do, well, not a darn thing. Who in the world thought that would be effective?

Our default setting is to sit, wait, and hope. If you're familiar with my stance of business growth and development at all, you know I believe that hope is not a business growth strategy. In fact, I'm clear hope is not a strategy for anything at all. You can read my blog post on exactly that right here: http://honoreecorder.com/hope-is-not-a-strategy/

So if we're not meant to sit, wait and hope, what on Earth are we supposed to do? The simple answer is *date*. Just as in personal dating, business dating is the act of getting to know our strategic partners so we can serve them and their clients and connections at the highest possible level, and the best way to do that is to intentionally and purposefully get to know them, over a period of time, until both parties feel comfortable about hiring and/or referring each other.

The obvious first date is coffee, lunch or an in-person meeting of some type. We all know about the first date: we go, we share our stories and what we do for our clients and customers, and we leave to go on about our business.

Then, well, pretty much nothing happens.

While we may have great intentions about following-up in a reasonable period of time, we dive into the waiting and hoping phase of networking. We're hoping the person we've met with reaches out to us in very short order to hire us, or with a plethora of referrals and introductions that will help us to meet our numbers with very little additional effort. And ... that almost never is the case. In fact, you shouldn't count on it happening at all. Ever.

Men know all about the act of dating. Many of my clients over the years have been married men, and to a person, they connected with the following analogy—

> *You lay eyes on a woman. After meeting her and taking her out on a date or two, you decide this is* the woman you will marry. *But you're not going to tell her that directly, you're going to court her ... take her out for drinks, lunches, dinners, movies, weekends away, eventually meet her parents and introduce her to yours. When the time is right, you ask her to marry you.*

Business dating is very similar, except that most people expect to get married after the first date, or even after the first initial ten-minute meeting at a networking event. Which, of course, in the dating world is the equivalent of picking someone up in a bar and asking them to go home with you ... right now. Can you see how this just isn't the most effective expectation you can hold about your networking meetings and business dates?

The Execution of Business Dating

Since we've established that waiting and hoping aren't effective, then I'm sure you want to know what is, and I'm going to tell you.

What you can do is take charge of the relationship, much like you are the man who has determined the woman he is going to marry. In business dating monogamy is discouraged, instead of encouraged. In fact, you're in search of 144 professionals with whom you share the exact same, or very similar, clients to put into your network and in your 12x12 Matrix.

Once you've had a positive first meeting, it's time to do several things to keep the momentum you've established:

- Send a hand-written thank you note. I'll talk more about this in the next chapter.
- Follow-up a week later with a phone call, to...
- Schedule your second date.

Now you're having your second date, and I've heard time and time again these second dates aren't likely to happen for two reasons:

- People feel like they've said everything they need to say at the first meeting.
- They have no idea what to say at the second meeting.

I know exactly what you're thinking: you don't know what to say to *set* the next meeting and you don't know what to say *at* the next meeting. Here's what you might not have realized: the second "date," and the subsequent meetings that will follow, are your opportunity to peel back the layers of your strategic partner to learn more and more about them.

What?! you're thinking. *I have to meet that person, who is just barely not a stranger, again?* Yes, yes you do.

"What do I say when I call them?"

I hear this a lot. Getting in front of your intended strategic partners is easier than you think.

Setting the Second Meeting

I'm working from the assumption that you had a terrific first conversation, and identified that your new

12x12 Matrix occupant is indeed a bona fide strategic partner candidate with lots of potential. Sweet! *Now what?*

I'm so glad you asked! You can email or call, and you can say a customized-by-you variation of this:

"I enjoyed our first conversation and think there's a possibility we could be beneficial to each other and our respective clients/contacts. If you're anything like me, I'm hesitant to make introductions without really knowing the person I'm recommending. I'm sure you're just as protective of your clients and connections as I am. I would really like to meet again and continue our conversation." Then ask if they are available next Tuesday {or whenever you're available}.

Or this …

"I really enjoyed our first meeting. I think there is a lot/some potential synergy for us. I'd like to get together to learn more about you and your business, and continue our conversation. How about next Tuesday over lunch?"

Simple. Easy. Direct. And … effective!

I advise you set the second meeting within two to three weeks of the first meeting with every single person who seems like someone you need to know better. Someone you've met just once will forget you faster than the person you intentionally follow-up with and meet with again in a relatively short period of time.

You don't want "out of sight, out of mind" to apply to you, so don't let it.

The Effective Second Meeting

I'm sure you have arrived at any second meetings feeling a bit awkward. Not unlike, perhaps, a real second date. I can relate. You're full of positive anticipation, yet unsure what the heck is going to happen next. Excellent!

Armed with the right tools, you will be an excellent second date and markedly improve your chances of moving the relationship forward. Rome wasn't built in a day, and neither are strategic partner relationships. You don't need to "close the loop" on where "the relationship is going" during the second date any more than you need to decide whether or not "tonight's the night" or you're going to marry the person you're personally dating.

Choose from this menu some second date options, topics, and questions that resonate with you. As you begin to recognize what works best for you, customize them to what works best for you.

Where To Go and What To Do

Getting together for your second, and subsequent dates can be as simple as meeting for a cup of coffee at Starbucks. Assuming you're up for an entire hour and a meal, you could invite them to your favorite lunch spot. I'm an early riser, as are many of my contacts due to our mutual dedication to *The Miracle Morning* practice {from the book of the same name by Hal Elrod}, so I've been known to have a 6 a.m. breakfast meeting. You can meet for drinks, head to an event like a Toastmasters meeting, Chamber of Commerce luncheon, BNI meeting, or even take in a sporting event.

Your deciding factors will include, but are not limited to:

- How comfortable you felt during your first interaction or two.
- What you know about your intended guest {i.e., you wouldn't invite someone of the Mormon faith to have drinks with you}.

Common sense and your level of comfort with each individual person should prevail. There's no rush to try to develop the relationship in a hurry, even if you are in a hurry. Take your time, do it right, and watch the results you're going after appear right before you eyes.

What To Talk About

Professional

- I want to really understand your business. *Ask a question that builds upon your last conversation.*
- Tell me about a recent positive client experience.
- What are your top three goals right now?
- If I were to put the perfect client in front of you right now, describe them to me.
- Depending upon the time of year, ask what promotions or campaigns they are engaged in.

Personal

- Tell me more about your family.
- Where did you go to school? Tell me about your degrees, experience, other education.
- How did you end up in *Austin, New York, Osaka?*
- Do you golf? Speak Spanish? Have a favorite or annual vacation destination?
- Where did you grow up?

What you need to know about your prospects and strategic partners is, well, everything. Not on the first or second or third or even tenth date. Over time, you'll want to learn all that you can. Finding common ground is the goal, because common ground is what gets you from "I don't know you, like you or trust you" to "I trust you enough to hire you, refer you and invite you into my life."

Just last night my husband and I attended the Inauguration Ball of the Governor of Texas as guests of friends and clients. During the drive home, one of our hosts was telling a story and said, "During that time, I was a personal trainer." This is something I hadn't learned about him in our more than fifty meetings. Now I have insight into why he's so fit! I also know a bit more than I did before accepting their invitation.

How Long Does This Go On?

Simple answer: until. Don't worry, I'll explain what "until" means sooner than later.

The "get to know you" process goes on and on and on. Hopefully it never ends!

Chances are, you dated your spouse until you both felt comfortable "going steady" or becoming exclusive. If either of you had put pressure on the other to move things along more quickly, the relationship might never have progressed at all.

Patience, my friends. Patience is a dish best kept warm, at a low temperature, until the time is right. In other words, if up until now you haven't been the most patient person in the world, the time has come for you to build that muscle until it is strong enough to withstand even the slowest-moving relationship!

BUSINESS DATING

In sales training sessions, I teach professionals to follow-up with a prospect until one of four outcomes occurs: *the prospect dies, goes out of business, sends a cease-and-desist letter,* or *hires you.* While this could take years, statistics show that closed business occurs most often after the seventh meeting. Eighty percent of sales require five follow-up calls after the meeting. Forty-four percent of salespeople give up after one follow-up. *Oops!* It isn't shocking why goals aren't achieved and objectives go unmet.

The same statistics hold true for developing strategic partner relationships. If you have multiple dates with a strategic partner, the importance of which is discussed in the next chapter, you exponentially increase the likelihood they will get to know you, like you, and hire or refer you. Your job then, is to stay committed to developing the relationship until they *change careers, move away, hire you, or refer you.*

This may mean you leave lots of unanswered messages, and send emails that never get a response.

Chalk that up to classic and rampant disorganization, not to *"I've done something wrong"* or *"They don't like me."* It is far easier to think you've done or said something wrong than to assume the person you're wanting to meet with is busy or a hot, disorganized mess when it comes to their networking and strategic partner development.

For the most part, professionals are not intentional and purposeful in their networking or in their day-to-day business activities for that matter. Far too many people wake up and see what comes at them during the day, rather than taking the day by the horns and making the most of it.

This will affect you because as much as your connections want to meet with you, see you, and refer you to their contacts, they are overwhelmed with their unending to do lists and lack of plan to accomplish the most important items on that list.

You must stay in the game to win the game. Simple as that. I'll cover more about the "how to" in the next chapter.

What To Share About Yourself, and When

As the author of *The Successful Single Mom* book series, one of the questions I get is, "When do I tell someone I have kids?" This is a logical question, and one that without question takes some thoughtful consideration. There is a school of thought that you wait to reveal you have kids when dating someone new, lest you scare them away. Personally, I'm of the school that you mention that right up front. I believe it's better to be authentic and open at the beginning.

Here's why:

You can't do the right thing with the wrong person. You can't do the wrong thing with the right person.

Having said that, common sense and logic must prevail in a new business dating relationship.

Just as there is such a thing as "too much too soon" in personal dating, the same holds true for business dating. If anything, it is even truer in business dating. Past personal dates won't be contacting future dates to warn them away from you. In business, a shake of the head or a few words of caution can end a potential relationship before it even begins.

You don't want to be the person who shares intimate details too soon, making the other person uncomfortable, or over-shares and risks offending the person in front of them. A bigger picture is in play here: your professional reputation. *People talk* – make no mistake: if you offend someone or hurt their feelings or gossip, others will hear about it whether they know you or not.

There are levels of sharing that you must observe, even as others may not, while building relationships. I have found that far too many people go "open kimono" {sharing way too much too soon} in initial meetings in an attempt to rush intimacy and secure the relationship while they have a live one on their hands. You must keep your overall reputation in mind as you build each and every relationship along the way, and use the big picture vision you hold in your mind as the guiding light for your conduct.

To that end, there are topics to avoid and waters you should just avoid testing at all costs.

Religion and Politics

Just like I don't share my political views with anyone other than my closest friends and family, I avoid "liking" posts I agree with, or posting my thoughts on Facebook. I avoid talking too much about my religious leanings, although I write about some of my thoughts and practices in some of my books.

I'm happy to listen to others' opinions and I'm actually curious about what others think and why they have come to the conclusions and adopted the beliefs they have, but I think it's best to keep my dial set on zipit.com unless I'm absolutely sure someone's thoughts and beliefs are in alignment with mine.

I recommend the same to you: avoid emotionally charged topics like politics and religion, and keep your focus pointed purely on topics that don't require discretion or caution.

Here are the topics you can discuss with almost reckless abandon, certainly with minimal filter:

- Your goals
- Your business or profession
- Your family
- Hobbies and interests

Having said that, my advice to my daughter is to never say or do anything she wouldn't want to appear on the cover of the *New York Times*. If you wouldn't want an opinion, point of view, or activity to appear front and center for the whole world to see, it's best to keep it to yourself.

If you find yourself receiving information that offends you deeply, or an opinion you vehemently disagree with, just nod and smile. Obviously you're the type of person someone else feels they can open up to. I can relate, I've been there many times myself. I've had people make egregious comments, offensive cracks, and share far "too much information" about themselves and their goings-on. I just listen intently, do my best to keep a smile on my face, and give thanks I am someone they feel comfortable sharing their opinions with.

Your Personal Brand

Probably one of the most overused phrases in job-hunting, networking and business in general is also one of the best and most underutilized strategies – *"dress for success."* Additionally, how you act, interact, and conduct yourself with others goes a long way to informing and influencing how people see you and whether or not you will get their business and referrals. I call this *"behaving for success."*

First impressions are crucial to your success, they truly are. Remember, you are marketing a product, yourself, to your prospective clients and strategic partners. The very first thing they see when greeting you is your attire. You must make every effort to show up in a way that is in concert with the business and relationships you are seeking. Otherwise, people can be left with the wrong impression about you, such as you are not sophisticated, educated, or knowledgeable enough to handle their business, and be a resource for them and their contacts.

Let's begin by discussing fashion and how it affects your personal brand. What we wear tells the rest of the how we feel about ourselves. Our attire conveys our income, level of education, and even defines our credibility. What we choose to wear sends a message to everyone we meet, without you ever saying a word. I would suggest you don't need to spend a lot of money or take up lots of time to pull together an acceptable outfit. Putting yourself together is a relatively simple undertaking that means you always look put together and professional, and it doesn't cost a fortune.

The phrase, *"Don't judge a book by its cover, see a man by his cloth, as there is often a good deal of solid worth and superior skill underneath a jacket and yaller pants,"* goes back to at least the mid-19th century, as seen in the newspaper *Piqua Democrat* in June of 1867.

The saying is also applied to people. How so? Well, people are often judged solely based upon their outward appearance. However, if we were to spend the time to get to know the person and see what's on the inside, we may be pleasantly surprised to find the person is very different than they first imagined. Hence, this expression is commonly used as a warning that a person should not judge people or things simply by what they see on the outside.

Unfortunately, the truth about the world, for better or worse, is that we *are* judged by our "cover." People make their initial impression and decisions about us almost instantly. Malcolm Gladwell introduces the concept of the "thin slice," in his book *Blink: The Power of Thinking Without Thinking.* The "thin slice" refers to the way that our unconscious minds can make what are in many cases highly accurate assessments in a very short amount of time, often a matter of seconds. Having this knowledge arms you with an edge: you can ensure you are well put together which will allow for you to get past the first stage of each relationship with ease and grace, and on to the possible great relationships that lie ahead. You can easily identify a wardrobe, which will ensure you are always well dressed, regardless of the occasion.

As Jennifer L. Scott says in *Lessons from Madame Chic: 20 Stylish Secrets I Learned While Living in Paris,* "Look presentable always." As I am not a true fashionista, I'll defer to the experts, and there are many great ones. You can read a few books, hire a personal shopper, or even engage a stylist to help you always to look and feel your best, but I advise you do at least one if not all three post-haste if you're unsure of how your personal presentation is, or is not, working for you.

Next on this short list of two is your business behavior.

BUSINESS DATING

As a coach, if I have a "job hazard" it is this: I see people engaging in activities that tarnish or even destroy their personal and professional brands, *and they aren't aware of it at all*. These same people, I believe, have a good heart and no malicious intent. But the results are the same, nonetheless. People avoid them, and doing business with them, like the plague. By being too aggressive, condescending, inappropriate, whining about business and/or life, or having a temper tantrum when things don't go their way, they ruin their chances of getting what they really want: great relationships and more business. Or, they fail to return calls or follow up in a timely fashion, leaving business on the table and their relationships shaking their heads in disdain.

I know I addressed the "what not to do's" in an earlier chapter, but this section of insight is entirely different. Behaving in business here is about how you are handling your day-to-day operations, contacts, emails, and other connections.

Here are some tips for getting your act "business behavior act" together, which will enhance how you feel about yourself, and how others feel about you:

1. Define a response time and stick to it. I'm always confused when I email or call someone and I don't hear back. Ever. {Or for weeks or months.} It tells me that the person is either {a} disorganized hot mess {best-case scenario} or {b} just downright rude {not good either}. If you have an inbox full of unanswered email, you must get a system in place and identify a response time you communicate. The same with phone calls: don't leave messages unanswered, even if you don't want the product or service being offered to you, or to have the meeting that was proposed. No is a complete sentence, and perfectly okay to say. I'd take a no over false interest or having to follow-up with someone indefinitely until I finally have to give up. Don't mess up a perfectly great situation by not responding in a timely fashion.

2. Be relational, not transactional. I've met some incredible people in the last few years, and some of them stand out in a fantastic way. They are warm and friendly and make everyone they meet feel special. Whether I hire them or not, I know they genuinely care about me which is such a great feeling. It also inspires me to want to do business with them the first minute I can.

On the other hand, I've met some folks who have dropped me a like a hot potato when they didn't close my business fast enough to suit their fancy. Guess what? Now that I know that's how they roll, I'm going to forever roll in a different direction. Look, some people have a longer "convincer strategy," which means they need more time to get to know you before they pull the trigger. Be patient. Be caring. Be awesome. It will be worth it, I promise.

3. People like assertive, not aggressive. I really dig a confident person who is comfortable in his or her own skin, easily shares their expertise, and is genuinely nice. That is really attractive, don't you agree? It goes without saying {actually, I guess it doesn't}, that you can "own your greatness," ask for the business you want, and get it. Just like that, too. Conversely, if you are too aggressive and pushy, that isn't attractive at all, and this is what will happen: *nothing.*

If you want business from people you're not getting business from, there's a reason and this might be it. The only way to truly know is to ask, and be ready for honest feedback.

4. Talk "to" not "about." Speaking of feedback ... if you have a problem with someone, talk *to* them, instead of *about* them. Here is what works better: "I have some feedback for you, if you'd like it." Or, "When you did/said X, I perceived it as Y. Is that what you meant?" Speculating only leads to false conclusions. If you're not sure why someone is doing something, ask them. If you think someone is intentionally doing something to make your head explode, ask them if that's the case. When you talk to others instead of directly to the person you have an issue with, you increase the negative feelings you have {which might be baseless, by the way}, rather than clearing the air. Sometimes one five-minute phone call can give you a new perspective and a clean slate.

5. Be "on" ... like a Wendy Elder. Someone I really admire for her consistently positive attitude and upbeat personality is a friend and strategic partner of mine here in Austin named Wendy Elder. She's a super busy real estate agent, business owner, wife, and mom. She never has a bad day and if she does, the world-at-large doesn't know about it. She carries herself with grace and poise, always has a smile, pays attention, and is good for an encouraging word. I was hanging with a girlfriend of mine, and she said, "This person I met is on, like a Wendy Elder." No, we weren't violating #4, these words were said with complete and total admiration, and I (1) knew instantly what she was talking about and (2) wanted to meet this person right away! Don't you want to be the person who is known for their awesomeness? I know I do.

Being perceived as an "on it" professional, and being dressed in a way that conveys confidence and professionalism isn't about perfection. It is about doing the best you can and continuing to grow into the person you've always known you can be.

We've come a long way. Soon you will be well on your way to building a solid and profitable network through effective business dating. But wait, there's more! Keep reading …

Chapter Seven:
What's Your Number?

"**L**et's get together … again, … and again, and again …"

Everyone has a number. Not their phone number, their "we've known each other long enough, seen each other enough times" number. Every person has a number of times they need to hear from you, see you, talk to you, and work with you before they feel comfortable referring you to others they know.

Here's the challenge: no one knows your number, not even you! That's right: everyone has a number, and no one knows what theirs is.

In order to get to the place in a relationship where someone is able and willing to go open kimono with you and give you their money, their trust, and their referrals, you have to stay on the Trust Bridge until you hit their number. And you have no idea how many touches that will take, or how long it will take.

Before I continue, there is one exception: you're a "one and done" type of person {meaning, it doesn't take more than one interaction to know for sure you want to move forward}. You're someone who knows what they want, and once they find it feel no hesitation about moving forward. My husband and I are both like that: we find someone or something we like, and we're either going to purchase or hire them right then, or come back when we are. Search concluded.

However, most people need to experience you a number of times before they are convinced you are the logical choice for their business, and even more times before you can expect to get their referrals and introductions. You are most likely the same way, wouldn't you agree? You need time to feel comfortable with another person, and there's no problem with taking the time it takes to feel comfortable.

Although I'm quick to make personal purchasing decisions, I'm fiercely protective of my clients and strategic partner relationships. I'm slow to move when it comes to my network, and it takes quite awhile for someone to earn those introductions. Even though I may hit it off with someone right away, most of the time I need a few conversations or meetings to feel comfortable.

Successful Business Dating Simplified

Let's correlate personal dating to professional dating in simple and general terms anyone can relate to, and everyone can integrate.

Author's Note: If you met your spouse on a Friday night, married them on Sunday, and have stayed together for twenty or fifty years *very happily*, while having several children who have all grown up to be multi-millionaires, then just know this: *you were born under a lucky star—and a huge congratulations to you!* You are the exception, a real-life in the flesh unicorn, not the rule. The following information is meant for the rest of us mere mortals …

Personal Dating – Date One

You meet a nice person you'd like to date. You go out to dinner and a movie, or even take things slower by meeting for a drink or some coffee. You discuss the basics: what you do for a living, where you went to school, where you've traveled, about life in general.

Business Dating – Date One

You meet a prospective strategic partner and hear them say something that piques your interest. You email or call to invite them to breakfast, lunch or coffee. Just like a first date with a love interest, you discuss the basics in addition to sharing how specifically you serve your clients or customers.

A successful first date, personal or business, means both people remain interested and intrigued by the other. By no means do you ask someone to buy from you, hire you, or refer you during that first conversation, any more than you'd ask someone to go home with you on the first date.

Asking someone to hire or refer you during that first real interaction is akin to saying, *"Happy to know you. Shall we hop in the sack?"* Even if you get the desired reaction, you've by no means developed even the beginnings of a solid relationship with positive potential. You have set the standard for a transactional relationship, not a mutually beneficial life-long relationship.

Personal Dating – Date Two

Building on date one, your goal during date two is to peel back another layer of the onion: you share a bit more, ask deeper questions, discover more about the person you're with, all while having a great time together doing something of mutual interest. You may think, "she's the one!" but it's too soon to know for sure. This is only the beginning, so as Ronald Reagan would say, "Trust but verify." If all continues to look good, you plan for another date.

Business Dating – Date Two

Your prospective strategic partner may have already showed interest in hiring or referring you, but this early in the relationship you must, as previously discussed, come from a place of giving first, be patient, and tread lightly. Just as in personal dating, the person you meet at the beginning may not be the person you get to know over a period of time.

Business Dating with Class, Finesse and Style

Beyond the second date, it's anybody's guess how quickly a deal can be closed or how long you'll have to be patient before you get to the best place in a relationship.

You will continue to meet for coffee, lunch, or drinks until the time comes when you take a weekend away in Paris, also known as "let's discuss our options for working together."

"I'd like you to meet my parents" is akin to "I have some people I'd like you to meet." These people include your business partners, colleagues, and other strategic partners, maybe even some prospective customers or clients. If the timing is right, you may feel comfortable making introductions to prospective clients, caveat included.

My standard caveat usually goes something like this: "I haven't known this person for a long time, but since we've met I've been impressed with … *her eye for design, his business acumen, his resume, her ability to get things done."*

Eventually you will be ready to ask, *"Will you marry me?"* also known as, "How would you like to pay for my services?" or "Who do you know that needs my services?"

Every relationship is built on multiple quality touches, and some relationships require more interactions than others. As you develop a relationship, you'll be in the excellent position to propose different options for getting together. They can include:

- Coffee
- Lunch
- Dinner
- Drinks
- Sporting events
- Networking events
- Charity functions
- ...and of course, many others.

As you are now an intentional business dating superstar, you'll suggest meeting places and events your intended strategic partner would find interesting, comfortable, and appropriate. In other words, you wouldn't invite a recovering alcoholic {if you're aware} to meet you at a wine bar. You wouldn't suggest golf to a non-golfer, but if someone expresses interest in learning to golf you can certainly pull together group golf lessons as a fantastic "get to know you" opportunity. You are mindful about asking someone to join you at church functions or other religious activities, at least until you have the necessary knowledge of their leanings.

Knowledge is power in general, and relationships are no different. What you will do in each and every meeting is ask questions that cause the person you want to get to know better to open up and actually let you get to know them better!

Then, you'll make and take notes so you can make the appropriate invitations in the future. Have a method for capturing the little gems of knowledge that come from each meeting.

Recently I met with a best-selling author I admire. In fact, I read the first book he wrote more than ten years ago. I met him a few months ago, and last week I found myself at breakfast with him discussing all things books, publishing, and goals for the coming year and upcoming projects. During our conversation, we also talked about our children, and I made note of his kids' names. We talked about our spouses, and I made note of his spouse's name and her vocation. I discovered by asking questions that we share similar philosophies on exercise, diet, and productivity. I even have the opportunity to find him a personal assistant.

Following our conversation, I immediately wrote him a hand-written note thanking him for his time and saying I'm looking forward to when our paths cross again. For a multitude of reasons, I intend to see him again and again and again in order to develop a mutually beneficial, long-term relationship. I anticipate, based on our mutual schedules and the fact that there's no real rush, our "get to know you" runway is quite long. And so the courting process begins. I have no expectation that next week all of the goodness that can come from this particular relationship will be realized. I do have the positive anticipation that over time we will develop a solid professional relationship and perhaps a personal friendship as well.

Timing Your Follow-up Like a Pro

Employing the 12x12 System and developing your 12x12 Matrix puts you in the driver's seat and in control of purposefully and intentionally developing your network. You get to decide who is worthy to occupy a spot in your Matrix. You choose how often to reach out and connect. You dictate the majority of the nuances surrounding the relationships because *you are the one in control*. You are the one driving the development of the relationship, at least for now.

When you have multiple connections in each and every category, that will mean you have up to one hundred and forty-four people to meet with, get to know, and attempt to refer business. All of those strategic partners and prospective strategic partners and their corresponding touches will leave you with virtually no time to worry if "that one person is going to come through with the deal that can make your year."

As I mentioned previously, if you let too much time pass between connecting, there are several things that can happen, and none of them are great! The longer you wait, the more awkward the encounter, the higher the chances the person you met has forgotten how fantastic you are, and worst of all, countless opportunities may be lost.

Because I know procrastination and the fear of rejection seem to reign supreme in professionals everywhere, what I'm about to say may seemingly "let you off the hook." It's not meant to do so, I mention it only to provide additional guidance regarding how often is too often, how long is to long in between follow-up attempts, and ultimately, how to get it "just right."

When deciding how often to follow up, I suggest you err on the side of waiting a little bit longer than you'd like to, but less time than you'd prefer. Let me explain.

When you have a terrific meeting, and you see the person across from you as a prime referral partner, you will want to meet with them again next week … or even tomorrow! I understand, I really do. But you have to keep in mind the person you've just met probably already has friends and strategic partners, and your enthusiasm could be mistaken for creepiness.

Don't be like the guy who texts twenty minutes after a first date ends to ensure you got home safely, and calls the next morning to wish you a happy day. *Too much, too soon.*

You'd be much better off sending a quick text or email the next day {I had a great time last night, hope to see you again soon!}, or even waiting a few days to check in. In business, as I mentioned previously, your best bet is to send a hand-written note expressing your gratitude for the meeting, and suggest another meeting again soon. Something like this:

Dear Bill,

It was lovely to meet you over breakfast today, thank you for taking the time to meet. I believe we have some potential synergy between our two businesses. Let's get together again soon and continue our conversation. I'll be in touch next week to get something on the calendar.

Sincerely, Martha

BUSINESS DATING

You look incredibly organized {note sent the same day}, gracious {you sent a hand-written note, which can be magical because notes are rare}, and professional. All of these are excellent qualities in a prospective strategic partner, which is what you've most likely just become for the other person.

You've had a good meeting and followed up at just the right time for the professional you've connected with to want to continue connecting with you. That was your outcome at the start, and that's where you can and should be with each person on your 12x12 Matrix.

The next question you might be asking is: *how do I effectively connect and develop relationships with the referrals I receive from my strategic partners?*

You'll employ the same strategies, slightly altered to match service provider status versus strategic partner status.

In the next chapter, I'll help you to formulate your strategy for success with prospective clients and customers.

Chapter Eight:
Know + Like + Trust = $$$$

In this book it has been established that "dating" the right people in business, in the right amount, with the right intention and expectation, can effectively and efficiently help you to reach your goals in record time.

What we haven't yet discussed is how to customize your follow-up system so you effectively stay in touch with someone until they are ready to engage with you in business and/or feel comfortable referring you on to someone who might be the perfect fit for what you're selling.

Let's ask the question. How do you know who is the "perfect fit for what you're selling?"

Wait, wait, I know this one! After much trial and error in several businesses, I decided to make it easy on myself and only work with the people who are in every way qualified, hungry, and excited for what I have to offer.

After much thought and deliberation, I learned valuable lessons, sometimes the hard way ... I put eight criteria in place and today these criteria help me to both qualify, and disqualify, prospective clients. When someone meets the eight qualifiers, I stay in touch with them *until* ... until what, you might ask? More on that in the next chapter, as promised.

Here are my qualifiers:

Coach's Note: Each qualifier is a building block, and one builds upon the next. If at any point one of the qualifiers isn't met, the person doesn't meet the basic criteria for a potentially successful and healthy working relationship and I usually abandon pursuit of their business.

- **You like them.** I used to be so enthusiastic about helping people, and I just *knew* I could help *anyone* that I didn't stop and think about how important it was that I really needed to truly like the person I was going to work with. The nature of my business is such that I truly must care about my clients and what they are going through in order to help them at the highest level. The same goes for you, and liking them comes *first.*

- **They like you.** Just as I must like my clients, it's important that they like me. You'll find that these first two qualifiers must be "present to win," i.e., if they aren't present, you're in for some trouble at some point. Better to let the relationship go, than to try to press on and make the relationship work.

- **You *know that you know that you know* you can help them.** This is a big one: I must know in my heart and soul I am the best person for the job, and that my skills, talents and abilities will absolutely help them reach their goals and objectives. It is so important you have the same conviction.

- **They *require* what you're selling.** In other words, do they *need* you, your products and/or services?
- **They have a *desire* (want) to hire or buy from you.**
- **They have *pain* you can prevent or eliminate, they have *pleasure* you can help them attain, or a void you can help fill.**
- **They have the power to make the decision to pay you, and/or they strongly influence the person (or people) who makes the final decision.**
- **They have the cash to easily, effortlessly, cheerfully, and willingly pay your price or fee.**

If and when all eight of these qualifiers are present, then you must stay in regular, intentional and purposeful contact *until*. As I mentioned, *until* has it's own set of qualifiers, so hang tight.

But first, a story:

I once worked with a headhunter for attorneys; I'll call her Melinda. Melinda's job was to recruit attorneys and their books of business to move to other firms, and find attorneys new positions who wanted to leave their current firms. She needed to connect with the managing partners of law firms, as they were at the helm of the decision-making process for most moves, as well as highly-marketable and profitable attorneys ready to make a move.

Prior to our working together, she had called a managing partner who said, "I'm not ready today, but in three months I want to hire two specific people." Three months went by, and then six. She phoned back after the six month mark {upon remembering she was supposed to call after three}, only to hear, "When I was ready to pull the trigger, I couldn't remember your last name or your firm name. So I hired another guy to do the job."

Fees lost: $225,000. *Ouch.*

I don't know where you sit on the income hierarchy, but that fees lost amount hit me right where it hurts ... and it wasn't even my loss!

Why did she lose that business? For two major reasons: {1} Because Melinda didn't have a follow-up system in place that triggered her to make the call as requested, and {2} she didn't have a separate "stay in touch" follow-up system in place that triggered her contact to call her when needed.

If she had called on schedule, she would have won the business. If she had failed to call, but still had a monthly email newsletter, her prospective client would have been able to lay his hands on her contact information at the exact moment he needed her services.

There are two lessons in there that you should consider putting in place as soon as possible: {1} have a plan to regularly follow-up with your connections "live" and {2} have a passive follow-up system that is a subtle reminder of you and your services. More on them in a just a moment ...

I'm going to suggest you learn from, and do, both in you pursuit of business. And a little bit more.

When I published *Vision to Reality* last year, I sent an email to past and current clients, as well as to many important connections and offered them a copy of the book in the format they would like the best {digital or paperback}. I sent copies of the book to some people I have known for more than a decade, but aren't in close touch with … just to let them know I was thinking about them and keep the relationship top of mind. One client, a managing partner of a law firm I started working with back in 2003, engaged me to do a large and lucrative project. He called after reading the book, we caught up during a quick ten-minute conversation, and I thought that was awesome {and the end of it}. A few weeks later, I received a call, *"Honorée, I've been thinking … "*

Although I had remained in touch with a once or twice yearly phone call, as well as weekly email newsletters, it was the book and note that got him thinking about working with me after a multi-year break. I believe that the constant contact had kept my skills and abilities in the back of his mind. Continually being in touch cemented my credibility, if nothing else through "staying power." People change professions often, some people change careers every few years … but here I am, after a decade, still coaching, speaking, writing books, and offering valuable content on a regular basis to my connections.

I write several books a year, which I talk about in my weekly newsletter. I also have a "street team" {a group of people who read the first final draft of the book before it's published … thank you street team!} that helps me to make sure the books are spot on. They receive advanced finished copies of my books. I also send the books to people in my network that I know would read and enjoy them.

Now I'm not suggesting that you write a book {and I'm not suggesting you don't – if you want to write a book, do it!}. I'm suggesting that there are creative and interesting ways to keep you and what you are selling top of mind. Ideally you want to be forefront in the minds of your strategic partners and prospective clients, so that right when they need you the most they know exactly how to reach you and hire you.

Keep the Love Alive!

There are the two systems, mentioned above, that need to be put in place to keep the relationship developing nicely. The good news? Both of them work in tandem with your 12x12 Matrix follow-up:

- Direct follow-up with prospective clients
- Passive follow-up with prospective clients

Direct Follow-Up

Direct follow-up includes anything you do to directly contact your prospective client; I call them "touches." Marketing tenants state that client acquisition requires seven to eight touches in the first sixty days in order for a client to engage or buy, and for a company to reach their annual revenue goals.

Touches are direct contact between you and your prospective client. They include:

1. phone calls
2. texts
3. coffee and lunch meetings
4. invitations to networking events
5. invitations for them to speak or be a panel member at an event you think would be right for them

As with your strategic partners, you must decide how often, past the initial seven touches, you want to be in touch with your prospective client in order to move the needle on the relationship and them closer to engaging you, your products and/or services.

In the initial stages, the emails, first meetings, and follow-up hand-written notes all factor in and are counted in those first seven touches.

If someone hasn't engaged at that point, you'll put them into your long-term follow-up. Have they given you a time it would be good to follow-up, such as after school starts or the first of the year? If so, schedule an appointment with yourself, including notes to jog your memory, so you'll follow-up at the precise time.

If they haven't provided the key info providing insight into the next-best time to follow-up, then you get to decide what works best for you. Initially, your follow-up will take place more often.

As the relationship progresses, there will be less of a need to stay in close touch. This is either because you have created a solid relationship, or there's only a need to stay in regular touch to keep the relationship on track, or because there isn't a strong connection. In the former case, reaching out every one to two months will keep the relationship progressing along nicely, and eventually you'll taper off to regular check-ins every three to six months. In the latter case, staying in touch every four to six months should do the trick.

There's no real science behind the right amount of time in between touches, you'll want to let common sense and logic be your guide. Having said that, you want to strike the right balance between staying in touch too often and appearing desperate and/or pushy, and not staying in touch often enough and missing potential opportunities.

Indirect Follow-Up

Long-term and on-going passive follow-up comes in to play in every prospective client relationship.

BUSINESS DATING

You'll want to adopt touches that keep you top of mind, develop the relationship and ultimately add as much value as possible. Just as face-to-face contact contributes to the strength of the relationship and ultimately informs your future client's buying decision process, passive touches contribute to the relationship by adding to your reputation, increase your standing as a credible expert, and help you to stand out as a professional.

These types of follow-up touches include these twenty tips that will passively nurture your prospective clients:

1. Forward via email the latest post of your monthly newsletter or blog letting them know you provide valuable information and ask them if they'd like to subscribe.

2. Ask prime prospects to write an article or include a quote for your newsletter on a topic in their area of expertise.

3. Set up Google alerts for information on your industry and send out a note on "What's Happening?" once a month.

4. Establish a community telephone call-in once a month. Speak on some relevant topic and open up the line for questions and answers.

5. Keep a calendar of birthdays, anniversaries, and special occasions. Pre-schedule cards through one of the online services such as Send Out Cards or JacquieLawson.com.

6. Create a postcard mailing for your entire list of prospects using a service like PostCardMania.com. Yes, I just said *postcards*. Some people notice them when they might not open an email.

7. Celebrate special events in their lives like a promotion, new job, new assignment, or new website, and send out a card or message using one of the resources from number five.

8. Make your prospective client smile – send them a light or funny note with a cartoon through a service like Glasbergen.com.

9. Send a "thank you for meeting with me" note and a thoughtful gift {such as a book, personalized notecards, or a nice pen}.

10. Divide up your list of prospects and send a "How are you?" or "Just thinking of you" note by email every day. You can take it up a notch by sending a handwritten note.

11. Send a substantive white paper, tip sheet, or advisory report twice a year.

12. Set your Google alerts for individuals and their companies. When you learn of news about these people, send an "I noticed ..." note.

13. Comment on your prospects' blogs, published articles or other promotional postings {such as on their Facebook Fan Page}.

14. Send surveys and industry information, links to podcasts or videos, and links to websites that offer free information that would help your prospects with their businesses.

15. Create your own industry survey using a service like SurveyMonkey.com. Send it to your entire network, publish the results and share in your email newsletter.

16. Write a testimonial about them or their product or service and submit it to them without being asked. You can also post a testimonial on LinkedIn. One note of caution: be sincere, authentic, and talk about an actual experience.

17. Interact with them on social networking sites such as LinkedIn, Instagram, or Twitter.

18. Invite them to be a short-term advisor to a committee in a relevant business association. They most likely will appreciate a shorter-term engagement and that you haven't asked them to be on a year long committee or Board.

19. Learn what causes or charities they support and make a donation (even if a small one) instead of a Christmas gift.

20. Follow your prospective clients contacts on Twitter and re-tweet their tweets.

Nurturing your network until prospects trust you enough to buy takes more than two, three, or even four contacts. How many contacts does it actually take? I've seen answers ranging from five to twenty or more contacts. But what keeps popping up most is "The Rule of Seven," which says that you must contact prospects a minimum of seven times in an 18-month period for them to remember you and feel comfortable enough to purchase from you. Most people seem to agree that it also takes seven contacts before they say "yes" to engaging in a new product or service.

Keeping your name in front of your network, and cementing the impression that you are an expert in your field is critical to increasing your revenue month over month, quarter over quarter, and year over year.

The Fortune is in the Follow-Up

Here's a common situation:

You've connected with a potential client, explained your services, and they seem excited to move forward. They even requested a proposal, and promise to review it and get back to you post-haste.

Then, nothing. Crickets. Maybe not even a cricket!

Weeks, even months, go by without a word ... no reply to emails, no returned phone calls, total radio silence.

What should you do? I mean, how long should you follow-up with someone who clearly doesn't seem as interested as you initially thought they were? You had a great conversation, they sounded enthusiastic, and you thought it was just a matter of a short time before they signed on the dotted line.

This is one of the main problems people face in business: lack of response from prospective customers and clients. Not wanting to seem too aggressive, professionals tend to give up after just a couple of attempts to close the deal. But this is the wrong strategy, in my opinion.

Let's look at it this way. Have you ever gone shopping for something a bit prematurely? You might have been gathering information, such as product cost, delivery time, the true quality or even expected results. Sure you have! You may have needed to wait for a big bonus or have enough time to save up to be able to afford to make the purchase. Or, perhaps like everyone else in the world, you are *busy*. You get the voicemail messages and think, *"I've got to call him back!"* only to immediately get distracted by what happens next. Or the email sits in your inbox just waiting for the moment you have the opportunity to respond.

Yes, you have. You've failed to respond to someone trying to get your business in a timely manner. Everyone has, including me. Now put the shoe on the other foot. This lack of response from prospective clients is not about you, it's about them. So, now let's answer the question: what should you do?

I say, *stay in the game*. In other words, continue to follow up, "until." The fortune is in your follow-up. I teach my coaching clients to continue to follow-up at practical intervals until one of four actions occurs on the part of the prospective client:

1. They die. Enough said.
2. They go out of business, or change their profession.
3. They send a cease-and-desist letter. That would be a "real" no.
4. They hire you. They refer you. They engage you. They buy from you.

Look, your prospective client is being ... well, *rude* by not responding. But that's probably not how they look at it. They might be, as you are sometimes, overwhelmed with work and life in general and just haven't had the time to give you the yes. Sometimes that's not it at all. Rather than take the time to say, "This isn't a good time." Or, "You're too expensive, I can't afford you." Or, "I'm still working to get approval," most prospects say nothing. They are probably thinking, "I need to answer and I have so much on my plate I'll get to it as soon as I can." Instead, they don't respond at all until they have a yes or some kind of definitive answer. This situation is a bummer for you, but when you accept it as reality and adjust your expectations and therefore your actions, you're in a much better position entirely.

You may follow up for months, even years. It took me seven years of follow-up and relationship development to land a client. They've now been a client for a half-dozen years, to the tune of six figures each year. Was it worth it for me to send multiple emails, go to countless breakfasts, make more phone calls then I can measure? You betcha.

If you know for sure you can help your prospect, you owe it to them and to yourself to continue to develop the relationship until they engage you. It will be worth the effort, I promise you.

Just as with strategic partners, the longer you stay in the game and focus on developing the relationship, the greater your chances for success, and that the relationship will monetize at some point.

Save the Assumptions

My final words on people who don't respond to your attempts to follow-up are these:

- Don't assume silence equals lack of interest. The worst thing you can do is stop following-up because you aren't hearing back. Stick with your follow-up plan for each person. *Until!*

- Keep reaching out. Timing is everything and you just don't know when the right timing is going to be. For every "one meeting and instant engagement" you have, you'll have a few eventual clients with much, much longer runways. Like I said, I finally landed a client after *seven years* because I stayed in direct and passive contact from the first meeting. I *knew* I could add value and results to the firm, and eventually I got the opportunity to do just that, and I'm still working with them to this day. Trust the follow-up process, it is meant to serve you.

In other words, stop saying, "I left two messages and sent an email, they must've changed their mind." Look, when you sit with a prospective client and you *know that you know that you know* you can help them, you owe it to them and to yourself to stay in touch and keep building the relationship because you know something they don't {about your product or service and how they can be helped}. You owe it to yourself because you chose your profession for a reason and the only way to be successful is to be consistent, persistent and patient. *Until.*

Chapter Nine:
To Know You is to Love, Hire & Refer You

I'm going to avoid any existential conversation along the lines of "how well do we ever know anyone, really," and instead keep our eye on the prize: *developing relationships that matter, relationships that are for the good of all concerned, relationships that are both mutually-beneficial and profitable.*

In addition to the strategies I've shared on how specifically to develop relationships, I think there are four personal performance cornerstones important in developing relationships. These cornerstones are intrinsically known, yet aren't talked about directly. These cornerstones, when practiced and observed, are fundamental to the success of any person's relationship development and staying power.

They are:

- Reputation
- Code of Conduct
- Discretion
- Friendliness

Reputation

Dictionary.com defines reputation as: *the estimation in which a person or thing is held, especially by the community or the public generally.*

Said differently, your reputation is what people say about you when you are not around. I've seen someone's reputation "ruined" with the shaking of a head or the furrowing of an eyebrow. Conversely, when the right person gives a ringing endorsement or simple nod of the head, multi-million dollar deals have occurred.

While it is impossible to please all of the people all of the time, it is your responsibility to behave in such a way that even if someone doesn't like you for some unknown reason, they can't really say anything "bad" about you, for the simple reason you live your life by a ...

Code of Conduct

Back in my early 20s, I adopted Jim Rohn and Napoleon Hill's advice to carefully consider, decide upon, and write down a code of conduct by which I wanted to live my life. It was a high aspiration, and not an easy one, at that.

When you have a code of conduct you have chosen to hold yourself to, most of the time you will be able to make decisions effortlessly. "Doing the right thing because it's the right thing to do" is a simple personal rule, yet having this rule prevents me from saying hurtful words, retaliating against hurtful actions, or acting in a way that could be viewed as {and this is the technical term}, "not good."

Just recently I found myself in a situation where lots of mud was being thrown around. Rumors were flying and assumptions were being made. I won't share the details of the situation, because they are unimportant. But I've held my tongue, recognizing the people making the assumptions and spreading the gossip wouldn't have been swayed by the facts. I believe this is true, in part, because they already had the proof and formed their negative opinion anyway. Also because it didn't seem to serve them to look at the situation logically, have a clarifying conversation, and then clear the air.

Not a problem for me, because I have my code of conduct to guide my actions and behaviors.

Following is Napoleon Hill's Code of Ethics, which I have slightly modified to suit me:

Napoleon Hill's Code Of Ethics

1. I believe in the Golden Rule as the basis of all human conduct. Therefore I will never do to another person that which I would not be willing for that person to do to me if our positions were reversed.

2. I will be honest, even to the slightest detail, in all my transactions with others, not only because of my desire to be fair with them but also because of my desire to impress the idea of honesty on my own subconscious mind, thereby weaving this essential quality into my own character.

3. I will forgive those who are unjust toward me, with no thought as to whether they deserve it or not, because I understand the law through which forgiveness of others strengthens my own character and wipes out the effects of my own transgressions, in my subconscious mind.

4. I will be just, generous, and fair with others always, even though I know these acts will go unnoticed and unrewarded, in the ordinary terms of reward, because I understand and intend to apply the law through the aid of which one's own character is but the sum total of one's own acts and deeds.

5. Whatever time I may have to devote to the discovery and exposure of the weaknesses and faults of others I will devote, more profitably, to the discovery and correction of my own.

6. I will slander no person, no matter how much I may believe another person may deserve it, because I wish to plant no destructive suggestions in my own subconscious mind.

7. I recognize the power of thought as being an inlet leading into my brain from the universal ocean of life, therefore I will set no destructive thoughts afloat upon that ocean lest they pollute the minds of others.

8. I will conquer the common human tendency toward hatred, and envy, and selfishness, and jealousy, and malice, and pessimism, and doubt, and fear, for I believe these to be the seed from which the world harvests most of its troubles.

9. When my mind is not occupied with thoughts that tend toward the attainment of my Definite Chief Aim in life, I will voluntarily keep it filled with thoughts of courage, and self-confidence, and goodwill toward others, and faith, and kindness, and loyalty, and love for truth and justice, for I believe these to be the seed from which the world reaps its harvest of progressive growth.

10. I understand that a mere passive belief in the soundness of the Golden Rule philosophy is of no value whatsoever, either to myself or to others. Therefore, I will actively put into operation this universal rule for good in all my transactions with others.

11. I understand the law through the operation of which my own character is developed from my own acts and thoughts. Therefore, I will guard with care all that goes into its development.

12. Realizing that enduring happiness comes only through helping others find it, that no act of kindness is without its reward, even though it may never be directly repaid, I will do my best to assist others when and where the opportunity appears.

To Mr. Hill's Code of Ethics, I added:

13. Leave everything and everyone better than I found them, and add value in any and every way I can.

I suggest, as did Mr. Hill, that you print out a copy and say it aloud daily until you've memorized it. This helps you to make these codes a part of you and will guide you in any and every important decision making process you encounter. You'll find it through the Napoleon Hill Foundation at NapHill.org and on my resources page at HonoreeCorder.com/Resources.

As a side note, I'm not suggesting you turn the other cheek to your detriment, fall on your sword no matter what, or allow others to treat you poorly. Nor am I suggesting that all of your thoughts, words, actions and behavior will fall perfectly in line because you memorize a few lines of text written decades ago. I'm suggesting that living a life above reproach puts you in an enviable position; one that means you won't be concerned about what others think of you or say about you – because it's mostly going to be great. And, if and when it isn't, you won't concern yourself about it for very long.

Discretion

Discretion, defined by Dictionary.com:

the quality of being discreet, especially with reference to one's own actions or speech; prudence or decorum:

is your ability to keep secret, important and/or highly confidential information to yourself. As a coach, I hear sensitive information in almost every coaching conversation. I have created an environment of transformation for each client, and transformation almost always requires sharing of one's biggest fears and deepest secrets. In that environment I'm told intimate, private, and highly personal thoughts and details that I am expected to keep to myself. Which I most certainly do. While coaching doesn't fall under a legal or ethical code of conduct that requires me to keep confidential information confidential in an "or else," situation, this is a strict standard I hold in my practice and it serves me well. My clients know they can tell me anything and it stays with me.

"Loose lips sink ships" is an idiom meaning "beware of unguarded talk." The phrase originated on propaganda posters during World War II. The phrase was created by the War Advertising Council and used on posters by the United States Office of War

Information. The gist of this particular slogan was that one should avoid speaking of ship movements, as this talk (if directed at or overheard by covert enemy agents) might allow the enemy to intercept and destroy the ships.

There were many similar such slogans, but "Loose lips sink ships" remained in the American idiom for the remainder of the century and has endured into this century for a reason. It is usually used as an admonition to avoid careless talk in general, and that's entirely my point: don't share information shared with you in confidence, whether you're asked to or not.

I share this for two reasons: (1) keeping confidential information confidential is an integral part of a strong relationship, and (2) I've known and worked with enough professionals that are legally and professionally bound to hold confidential information sacrosanct, *and yet they don't*. I've had confidential and classified information shared with me, and I'm not talking about during coaching conversations ... usually this not-to-be-shared confidential information is shared over coffee at Starbucks!

The people I meet with are in luck because I'm not going to repeat what I hear, and I'm not going to "report" them. But once a piece of secret information is shared with me, I know that I personally cannot trust them with any information I truly consider private, nor can I refer clients or customers to them.

If you've had something you've shared in confidence find its way somewhere you didn't intend, you know what I'm talking about. If you're the one who has broken someone's confidence {and who hasn't at one time or another}, I hope you have learned the lesson of keeping someone else's secret confidential without too much pain or suffering on anyone's part. It's important to be someone who can be counted on to be discreet. The qualities of being sensitive, prudent, judicious, and diplomatic ... not to mention protective of other's privacy, are great qualities to have and be known to have.

Trust me when I say others will know if you can keep a secret and they will also know if you can't and don't. Be someone who handles other people's information with as much care and concern as you handle your own {or better than you handle your own}! This practice of discretion will put you in the position of earning and keeping the trust of those key relationships you are working to develop, and will contribute to them being the long-lasting, mutually beneficial relationships you need to be successful.

Friendliness

How friendly are you? Indeed, being friendly is one of the elements of a relationship that does not cost money, but it's going to bring huge value to each and every encounter you have, and certainly to the relationships you're trying to build. A genuine smile that's part of an enthusiastic attitude, combined with real interest in the people we meet makes their day better. To that end, people do tend to spend more time with the people who make them feel good!

If you're not known for being friendly, I suggest you up your friendliness factor. Why? Being friendly builds relationships, and builds them faster than if you're just known as someone who's competent but not necessarily warm, easy to get to know and fun to be around. Friendliness enhances personal connections and can turn a budding relationship into something more meaningful. Effective Business Dating will mean you're going to spend hours attending breakfasts, lunches and evening meetings for the purpose of building relationships with other professionals, improving future contacts, and ultimately growing your business and revenues. Remember this: all the Business Dating in the world will not help you build a relationship of any lasting depth if you don't add some "serious" friendliness in there.

A High Friendliness Factor Adds a Positive Dimension to Your Relationships

Whether personal or professional in nature, being *friendly* can many times {okay, almost every single time!} be your ace in the hole. Think about it: if you have to choose between two people who do the same thing professionally, have the same level of competence, and virtually everything about them is identical BUT one is genuinely fun, fabulous and friendly, who are you gonna choose? Yup, me too. Here's why:

- Friendliness eases stress in tense situations. When there is a friendly atmosphere, people relax and are more able to be themselves. People in general are going to be less nervous or tense if they feel you are friendly. By being friendly, especially to someone you're just getting to know, you make it easy for them to feel comfortable around you.

- Friendliness can bring out the best in people. Being friendly encourages people to let go of any anxiety they are feeling, and be less self-conscious around you.

- Relationships develop faster, your connections will enjoy your company and try harder to help you when they feel comfortable around you. People will often bend over backwards when they like someone, they enjoy helping a friendly person, and you will find this is true for you, too.

- Friendliness improves overall confidence in a person and their abilities. People are happier to mix with others, take more chances, and are more motivated when they feel friendly towards each other. Everyone benefits. People can learn more about each other when they feel comfortable enough to open up.

- Complaints are few and far between, but when they happen are resolved much more quickly if the complainant has a friendly manner. In fact, if the complainant is met by a friendly, helpful person, the situation can be resolved much more quickly and easily. Think of an angry, irate customer, shouting and swearing, who is threatening in manner. They may well get results, but better results come from calmly explaining the problem and being friendly towards the person who is trying to resolve the matter. They are more likely to put themselves out and think of ways around the problem when they are treated in a friendly manner.

It seems hard to imagine that so much good can come from such little effort, but being friendly improves every area of your life, up and including your professional bottom line.

Cornerstones of Healthy Relationships

In addition to the four personal performance cornerstones, there are also the cornerstones of a healthy relationship. I'm going out on the skinny branches and declaring that it doesn't matter whether a relationship is personal or professional in nature, these qualities and characteristics impact the emotional safety each person feels within the relationship.

If, by chance, you don't think "emotional safety" is applicable to healthy business relationships, think again. Particularly because the nature of the work I do with people is incredibly personal, I regularly hear about breeches in trust, lack of feeling heard, not being prioritized, feeling misunderstood, situations lacking in necessary validation, empathy, even caring.

What is "emotional safety" in a healthy relationship? These are the degrees of security and comfort both people feel with each other. It's an integral part of a solid relationship foundation. By my definition, there are eight aspects in which to assess the emotional safety in a relationship. They are respect, trust, feeling prioritized, feeling heard, understanding, validation, empathy and love. If you easily excel in all of these areas, good for you! However, if you're like most people, there are areas that could benefit from some attention.

Take out a piece of paper and rate, from zero to ten, (zero being "never" and ten being "all the time") how well you feel you perform in each of the following eight aspects and descriptions of emotional safety.

1. Respect: Do you feel highly respected by others? How much do you feel you respect those around you? People who report low levels of respect often experience criticism or judgment from the other. Creating an environment of respect in each of your relationships is your goal.

2. Trust: Do you feel trusted by others? How much do you trust people in general? Many issues can spring out of a basic lack of trust, such as insecurity or doubt. Be someone others can trust and count on.

3. Feeling Prioritized: How high do you feel on others' list of priorities? How prioritized do you make others feel? "Being busy" and therefore having a slow response time can be truly detrimental to relationship building. Feeling low on the priority scale can lead to a build-up of resentment, which can be toxic to a relationship. Your fix? Prioritize others, even when you're busy {we're all busy!}. Make the time to reach out, check in, offer to be of service and add value.

4. Feeling Heard: How well do you feel others listen to you? On the flip side, are you a great listener? Those who don't feel heard complain of being ignored, tuned out, or talked over by the other. Develop your listening skills. I know it's harder for some than others, but really being a great listener gives you major points!

5. Understood: How much do you feel understood by others? How well do you feel you understand others? People with low levels of understanding from and of others report feeling high levels of frustration around people "not getting" them or feeling isolated instead of connected. Put yourself in others' shoes and try to understand where they are coming from, why they are acting the way they act and making the choices they make. Note: this doesn't excuse bad behavior, yet will work in your favor as you will be able to be proactive rather than reactive in many cases.

6. Validation: How well do you validate and show appreciation of those in your network? How much do you feel validated by each of them? Low levels of validation are problematic to any relationship. This is because both feel the other is rejecting their feelings, which causes and increases resentment. Validate others, even when you don't necessarily agree with them. Everyone likes to feel supported, and the easiest way to get support is to give it first.

Providing emotional safety in business relationships is key to your overall and long-term success.

Let Them Talk

Almost everyone loves to talk about their business if they own one. Everyone likes to talk about their profession, what they love and don't love about it. You're working toward goals that get you out of bed with enthusiasm and excitement every day {right?}, so share yours and ask about the ones your contacts have.

There are lots of sports fanatics running around {Geaux Saints!}, and I recently found out that one of my favorite clients, who is well into her 60s, still roots for her alma mater and was happy to discuss the football team's record for the year and their prospects for a bowl game and even the championship. You can connect over who won the Super Bowl, World Series, or Stanley Cup ... and if you root for the same team, you have the option of extending a timely invitation to an event that can cement your relationship like almost nothing else can.

A mutually-beneficial long-term personal or professional relationship literally requires you create an environment where all parties feel safe, supported, cared for, and genuinely liked. Using the tools in this chapter will help you to create the relationships you'll need to develop the business you desire.

Chapter Ten:
Business Dating for Ultimate Success

"You've read all the way through. Now you know what to do. So go on your way, go and prosper I say!" ~Honorée Corder {inspired by Dr. Seuss}

You've read all the way to the end of this book, and now you have a set of tools and strategies, that when you apply them, will indeed help you to create mutually-beneficial, long-term relationships. These relationships will enrich your life in ways you cannot possibly imagine today, as you read this.

I'm excited for you, because I know from personal experience what happens when you build a strong network of amazing relationships. I've been to birthday parties, weddings, open houses, visited exclusive islands, had behind-the-scenes tours of companies and institutions, and met people most others usually never do. I've prospered financially and in a dozen other ways because I've fostered connections with people over the years, all over the world. My gratitude for these experiences and opportunities won't be given justice here, in just a few words.

I also know from watching my clients build networks that have helped them grow their businesses to be profitable beyond their wildest imaginations.

I've seen struggling, on the verge of bankruptcy businesses turned completely around. I've seen socially awkward professionals trounce the former best networkers and rainmakers in their companies and firms, and go on to develop more business than they could handle {new problem alert!}. I've watched strong, independent and truly magnificent experts in their fields, at the top of their game, gain traction and take their results up a notch utilizing the tools in this book.

You might be thinking, "That's all fine and good for you and your clients, Honorée, but I'm different. I don't have the abilities you have."

I disagree.

Lest you are hesitant to put any of my suggestions to work, I want to remind you that some of the people you are closest to in this world, right now today, are the same people who were once complete strangers to you.

You met them in a classroom, at a bar, or on the street corner. You sat next to them on an airplane, met them at a conference, or joined the same networking organization. You were introduced by a relative, friend, or co-worker.

These same relationships that you cherish today were developed with the same strategies I outlined in this book – you just didn't consider them strategies, and you certainly weren't being strategic when developing them.

But you mean business now, don't you? And you want your business to thrive in the coming weeks, months and years. Right? I know you do!

Your future business depends upon you getting really intentional and strategic about each and every minute you spend *on* it, just as you are intentional about each and every dollar you spend *in* it.

If I know one thing, it's that you, like many of my clients, have probably spent far too long relying on things that are out of your control, to wait a moment longer to get smart about how you build your businesses. "Hope" isn't an effective business growth strategy. "Spray and pray," also known as handing out business cards to everyone and then waiting with a side of prayer, isn't an effective business growth strategy. Even going to every networking event you hear about isn't an effective business growth strategy.

I'm sure you're getting a kick out of those suggestions, now that you understand the ones that work, right?

Deciding who you want to do business with, your ideal client, is a great start. Identifying logical strategic partners and building win-win, long-term relationships is key. Creating, growing, modifying, expanding, and nurturing your 12x12 Matrix is a world-class game-changer, if I do say so myself.

The rest is up to you. It's time to get started!

<u>Gratitude</u>

To my husband, partner, and best friend, Byron.

To my daughter and inspiration, Lexi, I'm so grateful to be your mom.

To my mastermind peeps, Rich, Andrea, Scott, Jerald, Bill, John, Kim and Yoda ~ I'm so grateful for your support, ideas, and our synergy.

Big thanks to my advanced readers, editors and street team. You make every book better. You rock!

<u>Who is Honorée</u>

Honorée Corder is the author of a dozen books, including *Vision to Reality: How Short Term Massive Action Equals Long Term Maximum Results, Tall Order! 7 Master Strategies to Organize Your Life and Double Your Success in Half the Time, The Successful Single Mom* book series, *If Divorce is a Game, These are the Rules, The Successful Single Dad, Play2Pay*, and *Paying4College.* She is also a serial entrepreneur, keynote speaker, and executive coach. She empowers others to dream big, clarify their vision and turn that vision into reality.

Find out more about her at HonoreeCorder.com

Honorée Enterprises, Inc.
Honoree@HonoreeCorder.com
http://www.HonoreCorder.com
Twitter: @Honoree & @Singlemombooks
Facebook: http://www.facebook.com/Honoree

Additional titles by Honorée Corder

Vision to Reality: How Short Term Massive Action Equals Long Term Maximum Results

If Divorce is a Game, These are the Rules: 8 Rules for Thriving Before, During and After Divorce

Tall Order! 7 Master Strategies to Organize Your Life and Double Your Success in Half the Time

The Successful Single Mom

The Successful Single Mom Cooks! Cookbook

The Successful Single Mom Gets Rich!

The Successful Single Mom Finds Love

The Successful Single Mom Gets Fit!

The Successful Single Mom Gets an Education

Madre Soltera y Exitosa

Play2Pay: How to Save 25-50% on Your Child's College Education

Paying4College

The Successful Single Dad

Co-Author: *The Miracle Morning for Real Estate Agents* with Hal Elrod, Michael J. Maher, Michael Reese & Jay Kinder

20881464R00077